The Definitive Bull Terrier

(From Puss to Gully)

The Definitive Bull Terrier

(From Puss to Gully)

Frank Dyson

Also by Frank Dyson:

The Bull Terrier Handbook for Type, Conformation and Movement (1998)

Published by Bull Terrier Book Club
21 Rushyfield Crescent
Romiley
Cheshire
SK6 4LG

www.bullterrierbooks.co.uk

A CIP catalogue record for this book is available from the British Library.

Limited Edition of 250, Perfect bound, October 2016

ISBN 978-1-5272-0189-7

Book layout by Clare Brayshaw

Prepared and printed by:

York Publishing Services Ltd
64 Hallfield Road
Layerthorpe
York YO31 7ZQ

Tel: 01904 431213

Website: www.yps-publishing.co.uk

Contents

Introduction

Not another breed history book! As emphasised by my friends when I said I was writing one: "It's all been said before"; "there is nothing new to say" and "all you do to write a breed history book is get a couple of previous ones and copy what has already been written".

Well they would normally have been correct, of course. However, as an avid reader of Bull Terrier breed history books, I have always been left disappointed by unanswered questions, dead ends, grey areas that are never delved into and the biggest sin of the conformist, simply regurgitating what has been said before with little or no original research. So I set out to answer the questions that had always plagued me, review grey areas and prod dead ends with original research.

This work on the early history of the breed is called The Definitive Bull Terrier for a specific reason – it is the most authoritative and factually correct work on the early history of the breed. Why so – because it represents literally hundreds of hours of original research, digging deep into archive sources, that answers previously unanswered questions, rights wrongs, casts light on many aspects of the early history of the breed and, yes, it does re write some of the early history of the breed by definitively correct and verifiable facts not previously put in to print.

I had always thought it quite odd that we were expected to believe that a bulldog mated to a half bred bitch would produce offspring that apparently not only excelled in terrier rather than bulldog virtues but also and immediately began to breed somewhat "true to type" Hinks bull terriers. The brick wall default findings from the works of the conformists and internet searches always being that Old Madman was a bulldog who was exhibited and won the bulldog class at Birmingham in 1860. If I were faint hearted or less obstinate I would have given up and conceded defeat but it just did not ring true with me and that kept me going. Then, a breakthrough, then another – so I can provide readers with definitively correct and verifiable historic answers to the fable of Old Madman "the Bulldog".

The conformists write in various breed history books that James Hinks withdrew from the public show scene in 1870 but then no reasons are put forward for this other than, perhaps, pulling pints in his pub was more profitable than dog dealing and the reader is left none the wiser. I found this to be somewhat lame and research of events have disclosed that serious reputational incidents did occur in early 1870 that may well have combined and led to his withdrawal from public life for a period of time in 1870/1871 but then James Hinks did return from his exile to exhibit again. These matters are reviewed in detail.

As for the Puss fight, I found it very strange that we were asked to dismiss Rawden B Lee's account of the fight, penned some thirty years after the event but were then asked to wholeheartedly accept without question an alternative theory, put forward some one hundred and fifty years after the event, that there was no fight, that Bill Tupper did not own the Blue Boar and even that there was no Holborn show in 1862. What does this suggest about the respected Rawden B Lee – that his account, written in 1889, was a complete and utter fabrication from start to finish! Yes, Rawden B Lee's account was put to paper some thirty years after the incident. Yes, it may have been passed by word of mouth and some of the facts certainly confused but, as we will see, the basic premise that there was a fight at Bill Tupper's Blue Boars Head in Long Acre appears, on the balance of probability, to be correct.

The second Holborn Horse Repository and dog show in 1862 has caused much controversy and confusion for bull terrier enthusiasts and breed historians, many of whom have tied themselves in knots, so this matter is also cleared up with definitively correct and verifiable historic answers. Research into the Puss fight has also enabled a light to be cast for the first time on some of the strong individuals who formed part of the London school of "old doggy men" together with Hinks's unfruitful dalliance with them and an in depth review of one of them – that being William ("Bill") Tupper, whom Hinks first exhibited against in bulldogs at a London show organised by the London school of "old doggy men" in the first week of October 1861.

I also found it quite intriguing that, with regard to the sons, Frederick and James Jr, Frederick Hinks was to a very large extent pencilled out of modern breed history books by reference merely to dogs owned by "Hinks" and owned by the "Hinks family" without naming Frederick but otherwise naming the dogs owned by James Jr. Neither James Jr nor his son Carleton gave any credit to Frederick. An example of this is James Jr writing: *The all white Bull-terrier was founded by my father, James Hinks, of Birmingham... My father died in 1878 and after his death I carried on until some few years ago I handed over the reins to my son, Carleton.* No mention by James Jr of his brother Frederick. However, research clearly shows that it was Frederick who immediately took over the mantle from his father and that he deserves some specific credit in the development of the breed on both sides of the Atlantic and the continuation of the influential "Hinks line" up to the 1900's.

The origin of the Bull Terrier lies embedded in the Bulldog, so this work commences with a quick run through of the history of the Mastiff and Bulldog, the Monarchs of the day, sporting pastimes and the sporting raconteurs of the 1850's and 1860's, all of which sets the scene for the Puss fight at Bill Tupper's Blue Boars Head in Long Acre.

Monarchs and Mastys

The antiquity of the Bulldog is unquestionable, having been developed from the Mastiffs who came down from the ancient alauntes. Mastiffs had been used for bear and bull baiting prior to 1066. We know this as a fact because the Domesday Book, instigated by William the Conqueror in 1086, refers to the town of Norwich having paid sums of money to King Edward the Confessor and the Earl of Norwich for *six sextaries of honey, a bear and six bear dogs.* King Edward died in 1066 and was succeeded by King Harold II, who died at the battle of Hastings in the same year. Part of the Bayeux Tapestry depicts King Harold on horseback with a group of large type dogs around him. William the Conqueror had a great love of sport. It is said that *he took away much land from God and men and converted it to the use of wild beasts and the sport of dogs.*

As far back as Roman times, the dogs of Britain were held in high esteem for war, in the arena, and hunting. During the Anglo Saxon age, hunting was the chief recreation of the Kings and English Monarchs held great sway over the peoples of the land. Prior to William the Conqueror, King Canute (1016 – 1035) allowed every freeman to sport on his own land and Edward the Confessor (1042 – 1066) confirmed this law but enforced the death penalty for hunting on Crown land. William the Conqueror and his sons added to these regulations protecting Crown land under the Anglo Norman forest laws. The problem for the ordinary folk wishing to utilise land for grazing, forage and to put food on the table of their family was that whereas the Domesday Book recorded 5 forests, others were later declared by various Monarchs as Crown land and even more forests were being made such that, by 1199, the greater part of the realm was entirely forested. "Forest" did not necessarily mean areas covered with trees, it included fields, moors and sometimes encompassed farms and villages.

Prior to the Norman conquest, forest laws were directed at protecting the Royal game from commoners dogs: *no mean person may keep any grey-hounds but freemen may keep grey-hounds so that their knees be cut........*The only dogs allowed in a Royal forest were small "lap" dogs *because in them there is no danger and therefore they shall not need to be hoxed or have their knees cut.*

The Normans extended the control of dogs as they increased the amount of Royal forest, Henry I, the youngest son of William the Conqueror who ruled from 1100 – 1135, extended the maiming of dogs to those that lived outside the forest, by having one of their claws chopped off. Henry II declared under the Laws of the Forest *that every man dwelling within any forest might keep a mastiff about his house for the defence of it and his goods, if it was lawfully maimed or expediated.* The Kings noblemen, favourites and Abbots were often exempted from having their dogs maimed: *Let no one maim the dogs belonging to the household of an Abbot and his Monks, but let the Abbot and his Monks maim the dogs of their own men dwelling in the forest.* This persecution of commoners dogs continued and King John who ruled from 1199 – 1216, not only rigorously enforced the existing game laws but added to them. He not only created more Royal forests but is said to have *ordered all dogs and mastiffs in every forest in the Kingdom to be slaughtered.* Thus, when King John received his comeuppance, the Charter of the Forests was issued as a complimentary charter to the Magna Carta. The forest charter required that some Royal "forests" were relinquished and it provided real rights, privileges and protections for commoners, including the right to forage for food and graze animals. The death penalty for killing deer was also repealed, replaced by fines or imprisonment. Dogs in and around the forest were still maimed, by cutting out the ball and having three claws of the right foot cut off.

The English Mastiff had always been well regarded as a dog of war. Sir Piers Legh was wounded in the Battle of Agincourt in 1415 and it is said that his Mastiff stood over him and protected him throughout the remainder of the battle. In 1518, Henry VIII sent 400 mastiffs, garnished with spiked collars, as a gift to Charles V of Spain for use as war dogs against the French. Elizabeth I also sent Mastiffs as part of a contingent of troops with the Earl of Essex, then Lord Deputy of Ireland, to put down an Irish insurrection in 1599. The Essex expedition was a failure, the mastiffs little used and the Earl lost his head.

In fact we have Queen Elizabeth I, as a great supporter of the Mastiff and sporting dogs. When confined by her sister Mary at Hatfield House, she was entertained *with a great exhibition of bear baiting with which their highnesses were right well content.* In 1559, the then Queen Elizabeth entertained French Ambassadors *and after dinner they were entertained with the baiting of bears and bulls with English dogs.* When the French Ambassadors visit ended they went away *and carried with them many mastiffs given them, for hunting their wolves.* In the "Survey of London" written by John Stow in 1598, it is recorded that there were two Bear Gardens, the old and the new, *wherein were kept Bears, Bulls and other Beasts to be baited. As also Mastiffs in their several kennels are there nourished to bait them.*

In 1591, an order was made prohibiting the exhibition of plays on Thursdays because on that day bear baiting and other such like pastimes were practised: *Tomorrow being Thursdaie, shal be seen at the bear-garden on the Bankside, a greate match plaid by the gamesters of Essex, who hath challenged all comers whatsoever, to plaie 5 dogges at the single bear, for 5 pounds; and also to wearie a bull dead at the stake; and for their better content, shal have pleasant sport with the horse and ape, and whipping of the blind bear.*

So popular was bear baiting that the Master of the Bear-Garden in Queen Elizabeth's time was also allowed to have public baitings on Sundays and this continued until stopped by James I in 1618. James I was not against baiting, apart from Sundays, as he baited Lions regularly in the Tower of London with Mastiffs, for his own amusement.

As can be imagined, such regular amusements would go through a great deal of dogs and a ready supply was therefore required. Hence, the Master of the Game was granted the most unlimited authority to issue commissions and to send his officers into every county of England who were empowered to seize and take away any bears, bulls, or dogs that they thought fit for the purpose. This power was often abused and in order to avoid such indiscriminate seizing of local dogs the authority in some places promised to send to the Master of the Game a certain number of mastiffs each year.

There is an excellent summary of the Elizabethan sports contained in "A Journey into England" written by Paul Hentzner in 1598. This book is said by some to be the earliest known use of the word "Bulldog". However, this is patently incorrect. The original words in Latin used by Hentzner were *Moloffis Anglicis,* which is a definite reference to "English Mastiff". The translation of the book into English was not made until 1757, by which time the Bulldog had superseded the Mastiff in these sports and the translator used the word of his time "Bulldog" rather than, for the time of Hentzner, the more correct "Mastiff":

> *There is still another place, built in the form of a theatre, which serves for the baiting of Bulls and Bears; they are fastened behind, and then worried by great English Bull-dogs[sic]; but not without great risque to the dogs, from the horns of the one and the teeth of the other; and it sometimes happens they are killed upon the spot; fresh ones are immediately supplied in the place of those that are wounded, or tired. To this entertainment, there often follows that of whipping a blinded bear, which is performed by five or six men, standing circularly with whips, which they exercise upon him without any mercy, as he cannot escape from them because of his chain; he defends himself with all his force and skill, throwing down all who come within his reach and are not active enough to get out of it, and tearing the whips out of their hands and breaking them. At these spectacles, and everywhere else, the English are constantly smoking tobacco. The general drink is beer, strong, and what soon fuddles.*

Breed history and other dog books quite often quote "Caius" when reviewing the origins of the dog. This was, in fact, Dr John Kaye who was physician to three sovereigns, Edward VI, Queen Mary and her sister Queen Elizabeth I. In his treatise De Canibus Britannicis (Of English Dogs), written in Latin and translated into English by Abraham Fleming in 1576, Dr Caius refers variously to *the Mastive, or Bandogge, the Dogge Keeper or watchman, or Tydogge.* These are all names for the same type of dog, *because manie of them are tied up in chaines and strong bonds, in the dai time, for doing hurt abroad, which is a huge dog, stubborne, ouglie, eager, burthenous of bodie, of little swiftness, terrible and fearful to behold.....They are appoynted to watche and keepe farme places and country cotages sequestred from common recourse, and not abutting upon other houses by reason of distaunce, when there is any feare conceaved of theefes, robbers, spoylers and night wanderers. They are serviceable against the fox and the badger, to drive wilde and tame swyne out of medowes, pastures, glebelands and places planted with fruite, to bayte and take the bull by the eare, when occasion so requireth. One dog or two at the uttermost are sufficient for that purpose.....For it is a kinde of dogge capeable of courage, violent and valiaunt, striking could feare into the harts of men, but standing in feare of no man, in so much that no weapons will make him shrinke, nor abridge his boldness..........some barke and bite not. Some bite and barke not.*

Bulldoggs

The first use of the word Bulldog in the English language (as opposed to writings in latin that have been translated into English) appear in letters from a gentleman called Prestwick Eaton, when writing from his home in St Sebastian to his friend George Wellingham, in 1631 and 1632. He asked for *a good mastiff dog, his case of bottles replenished with the best lickour, and pray procure mee two good Bulldoggs and let them be sent by first ship.* It is most interesting that Mr Eaton mentions the Mastiff and the Bulldogg in the same letter, which would indicate that they are clearly, by 1632, acknowledged to be separate types of dog.

The original Bulldog was most probably a short faced mastiff type as related by John Houghton in 1694 when describing a bull bait:......*the bull circulates to watch his enemy, which is a mastiff dog (commonly used to the sport) with a short nose, that his teeth may take the better hold. This dog, if right, will creep upon his belly, that he may, if possible, get the bull by the nose, which the bull as carefully strives to defend, by laying it close to the ground.*

In course of time, the Bulldog was reduced in size with the aim of producing the highest courage with the smallest amount of physical power that could pin a bull: *the lowering eye, somewhat projecting and heavy jaw; broad massive, round skull, distended nostrils and, in some cases, teeth constantly exposed; together with his deep, ample and muscular chest, gave this redoubted and formidable animal a terrific aspect not belied by his undaunted courage and invincible obstinacy in combat. He rarely barked or even growled, but attacked in silence and in front.* It was clear that there was a crossover point at some time between the mastiff and the bulldog, as it was written: *The true-bred masty shows not his teeth, nor opens, till he bites.*

The Rev Daniel in his book "Rural Sports", published in 1802, relates that Bull baiting was recorded as an event held at Stamford in Lincolnshire as early as 1209 and in Tutbury in Staffordshire around 1374. Bull running and baiting was an annual event at Tutbury, however, this was not a rag tag event. There would first be a church service, followed by dinner. The bull would then be provided by the bailiff of the manor and would thereafter be prepared for the run by having the tips of its horns cut off, its ears and tail cut off, its body smeared with soap and beaten pepper blown into its nose. Only minstrels were allowed within forty feet of the bull which was pursued through the streets and fields of the priory. It was the task of the minstrels to cut off a piece of the bull's skin before it crossed the boundary between Staffordshire and Derbyshire. If they did so, then the bull was captured and taken to the bull-ring in Tutbury and baited with dogs. If the bull made it across the boundary into Derbyshire, it again belonged to the bailiff of the manor. At some time local county rivalries intervened to upset the gentlemanly order of the day: *the young men of Stafford and Derbyshires contend with cudgels about a yard long, the one party to drive the bull into Derbyshire, the other to keep him in Staffordshire, in which contest many heads are often broken.* It may be that this, together with the general distaste that developed amongst the gentry for such events, served to bring the event to an end at Tutbury around 1778.

Bull Runs were held at Stamford annually on the 13th November (unless it was a Sunday when the Run would be the following day). A detailed "eye witness" report of a Bull Run held there on 14th November 1825, was provided in Hone's Every Day Book of Popular Amusements: *"It is conducted with a most determined spirit and unlike most other customs seems to increase in notoriety yearly.... the bull running is a sport of no pleasure, except to such as take a pleasure in beastliness and mischief. It is performed just the day six weeks before Christmas. The Butchers of the town at their own charge purchase a wild bull, this bull overnight is had into some stable or barn belonging to the alderman. The next morning proclamation is made by the common bellman of the town, round about the same, that each one shut up his shop doors and gates and none, under pain of imprisonment, do any violence to strangers, for the preventing whereof (the town being a great thoroughfare and then being in term time) a guard is appointed for the passing of travellers through the same without hurt. None to have any iron upon their bull clubs, or other staff which they pursue the bull with, which proclamation made and the gates all shut up, the bull is turned out of the alderman's house and then, hivie, skivy, tag rag, men women and children, of all sorts and sizes, with all the dogs in the town, promiscuously running after him with their bull clubs, spattering dirt in each others faces, that one would think them to be so many furies started out of hell for the punishment of Ceberous....a ragged troop of boys and girls do pillow him with stones, with clubs, with whips and many nips, they part his skin from bones."*

Most sizeable towns in the 17th and 18th centuries had bullrings where bulls had to be baited by law before they were allowed to be slaughtered for beef. This was said to tenderise the beef. Butchers could and would be prosecuted and fined for the offence of slaughtering unbaited bulls. For bull baiting, there was no doubt that a smaller dog of not more than, say, 50lbs would be better suited than a larger one because the bulldog would approach the bull low with its belly close to the ground. A large dog would be more likely to be caught by the bull's horns than a smaller one. However, from being a spectacle practised in many towns nationwide, bull baiting turned into a very cruel enterprise for the amusement of the masses. If the bull was flagging stimulants were, for example, to pour boiling water in its ear or, if it were lying down through exhaustion, to set fire to straw placed beneath it. The dogs also suffered terribly in their cruel owner's mutilation of them to show how tough they were. Take this extract from the KC Stud Book of 1874 for evidence, tracing back the pedigree of one particular Bulldog: *Bratton's Peter (who pinned the bull on his raw stumps after his feet had been cut off one by one by his owner, for a wager).*

An Act for the legal protection of animals was introduced in the House of Commons in 1822, championed by Irish Member of Parliament Richard Martin. The Act became known as the Martin's Act and made it a crime to treat a handful of domesticated animals such as cattle, oxen, horses, and sheep cruelly or to inflict unnecessary suffering upon them. However, due to the narrow terms and precise wording of the Act, it appeared quite useless at stopping bull and other types of baiting and fighting.

From James I, baiting lions at the Tower, the last recorded contests between lions and dogs in England took place at Warwick in 1825, whereby a Mr Wombwell, who travelled the country with a menagerie of wild animals in cages, advertised the events.

To put it in perspective for the reader, this travelling menagerie contained *"Three other lions, a she wolf with cubs, a hyena, a white bear, a lioness, two female leopards with cubs, two zebras, a large assortment of monkeys and two wild asses...."* Two lions were to be put up for baiting, Nero, who turned out to be apparently tame and quite docile to the extent that Mr Wombwell was able to enter the cage on more than one instance to give Nero water and inspect his wounds and Wallace, who was much more ferocious to the extent that his keepers could not enter his cage at all. According to Enno Meyer in his book, The Bulldog, published in 1948, the dogs used in the lion baiting were supplied by Ben White of Kensal New Town, North London. An agent for Mr Martin applied to the local authorities to stop the exhibition. However, the local magistrate declined to intervene on the grounds that, under Mr Martin's present act, no steps could be taken before the act constituting cruelty had been committed. I do not believe that it adds to go into detail of the contests, which can be found in various books, suffice it to repeat the conclusion reached that: *It is not possible to find more striking and conclusive proof of the indomitable and reckless valour of the dog, even when combating against overwhelming odds, than is demonstrated by those descriptions; neither would it be very facile to meet with instances in which the courage of that generous creature (given for the protection of his master, man) has been more disgracefully abused by him, to whom his sagacity, bravery and a host of virtues are devoted with the uttermost abnegation of self.*

So the bulldog became almost entirely owned by the roughest classes of society, the more refined classes finding such sport of the lower classes most distasteful. This view was confirmed by William Taplin in his book, published in 1803 and grandly entitled "The Sporting Dictionary and Rural Repository of General Information upon every subject appertaining to The Sports of the Field" wherein he wrote:

> *A bulldog, though inoffensive and harmless when properly domesticated, forms to the eye of timidity a most terrific appearance; the doubtful and designing leer of the eye, the tiger like shortness of the head, the under hung jaw, the wideness of the forehead, the width of the skull, the distension of the nostrils and the almost constant sight of the teeth hold forth a very emphatic specimen of the power they possess when that power is brought into action. The breed is by no means so numerous as formerly, in consequence of the gradual decline of bull baiting and the great number taken abroad, for many of which very great prices were obtained. The natural ferocity, strength and thirst for blood in this animal rendered them a formidable nuisance in their unrestrained state and they are now seldom seen at their full liberty, either in town or country, the owners, from a proper fear of the law, finding it most prudent to keep them properly confined.*

Bull baiting was finally forbidden by the Cruelty to Animals Act of 1835, although it was said to have been continued illegally for several years in various places, particularly around the West Midlands and Staffordshire. As recounted by Taplin, the pure Bulldog was becoming a rarity in the early 1800's and the Cruelty to Animals Act brought about a further decline in the Bulldog for, without bull baiting, they served no useful purpose to those that previously owned or traded them and the public had no wish to own such ferocious dogs, generally in the company of cruel scoundrels.

If it had not been for the true Bulldog enthusiasts, the breed would probably have died out. Nevertheless, Bulldogs remained in the doldrums until the showing of dogs at sporting houses in the 1840's enabled a more refined Bulldog to be put in front of the public. These Bulldogs retained their trademark physical features but with a diminished aggressive nature, which did much to reverse the prevailing prejudice against them.

Edward Ash in The Practical Dog Book, relates that J H Walsh (Stonehenge) became editor of The Field in 1857 and that Walsh had no love for the bulldog, describing them as creatures entirely lacking in all canine virtue. Perhaps Mr Walsh came under some pressure from bulldoggers because he changed his view of the bulldog but then voiced his disdain of the bull terrier: *Experience has shown us that these dogs are not capable of much attachment; that they are not safely to be trusted; that they are very rarely, if ever, teachable; but that, in a general way, they are gentle and quiet in their demeanour. A dog of this breed is not quarrelsome, he is a capital guard or watch dog and certainly ought to be looked upon as an invaluable animal for instilling courage and endurance into any description of dog requiring such properties, by direct or partial crosses. He is pre-eminent amongst the canine race for the following qualities: he attacks silently; he bears any amount of punishment without uttering a sound; he invariably goes at the head of his adversary and he will not let go until he is killed or made insensible by strangulation. For these properties, especially his forward attack and holding powers, he was selected to bait the bear, the bull and occasionally the lion for, although the half bred dog might almost equal the genuine animal in courage, it was always doubtful whether a bull terrier*

would seize the head or the heel and, as a celebrated old bull baiter impressed upon us some years ago "pinning is winning when you loose a dog at a bull". Stonehenge's opinion of the bull terrier did soften as time went on though.

Walsh judged the Bulldog class at the Birmingham show in 1860, where James Hinks won the class but Walsh's critique on Hinks's winning animal still showed a certain disdain for the breed.

Sporting Pastimes

Charley Aistrop was the story of legends, born into a respectable family, as a young gentleman he followed his passion of sporting dogs, with one of his dogs winning a prize at a bull baiting. This did not go down very well at home and he was given the choice of either giving up the dog fancy or leaving the house, apparently having seven days to arrive at a decision. Charley did not need to take a week, in the very next sentence he bade his goodbye. His mother, seeing his determination but also considering the honour of the family name, sent him on his way with a hundred guineas in his pocket. Charley Aistrop became, perhaps, one of the most famous sporting raconteurs of the 1800's, setting up business at the Cock Pit, Duck Lane, Westminster.

Bear baiting remained popular and was carried on in sporting drums up to the advent of the Cruelty to Animals Act of 1835. In fact, the bear was to be the downfall of the famous Charley Aistrop and his infamous Westminster Pit. Mrs Aistrop was killed by a bear which was kept at the Westminster Pit for baiting – the bear attacked and killed her whilst she was feeding it. When Charley arrived at the Pit, he discovered the deadly deed, killed the bear and, shortly after, sold Westminster Pit, becoming a more respectable licensed victualler. He remarried and died in 1859 and a dog show was organised with donations for the benefit of his widow.

It is quite difficult these days to get our head around the fact that our forebears nationwide either loved to "try out" their dogs or loved to watch others "try out" their dogs. This went on for a good 500 years and more. As time progressed, owners would deliberately mutilate their dogs either to give them a "tough" appearance or to "improve" their performance at the sport. The cords which connected the lips to the gums would be cut and the foreface of puppies would then be driven back by cruel use of blocks and clamps. Nasal sinews were cut and the pendulous flews cut off. These "improvements" were designed to allow the dog to breathe more freely whilst holding on to the bull. Dogs used for fighting would have their ears entirely cut off. Many breeds traditionally had cropped ears, which was deemed to be a more aesthetic appearance, bringing the ear to a sharp point, with the outer edge concave in outline. Courage and fearlessness were bred for with no regard at all for aesthetic points and gameness was the common factor. It goes without saying that only the most courageous and ablest of these dogs survived to breed and, as put succinctly by Mr R H Glyn, that *no domestic "pet" has been so severely tested or so consistently bred for one characteristic.* The result was that British bull breeds gained a worldwide reputation for courage, steadfastness, an obedience to the whim of their master and un-dying loyalty.

In the second half of the 18th century, dog fighting became more popular and began to interest the gentry. This would have served to increase the wagers and consequently the value of the successful dogs and their progeny, giving a greater reward to the breeders/dealers in the combatants of the sport. The bull-terrier superseded the pure bulldog in the pit where it was quicker and consequently got hold first. It is said that the bull-terrier also had a greater strength of jaw than the bulldog of the day, whilst displaying equal tenacity and courage.

The bull and terrier or bull dog terrier was the result of crossing the then bulldogs with the then terriers, creating the original bull and terrier. The aim being to produce a fearless dog impervious to pain to undertake the tasks of the day, these being fighting, baiting, drawing and ratting. Badger baiting was a common practise. In the "sport" of drawing, a dog was required to enter a cage, approximately seven feet long, in which a badger had been placed. The dog had to grab the badger and draw it out of the tunnel. Bets were placed and the winner was the dog that could accomplish the task in the quickest time or the most times in a given period. At each attempted draw, the badger would become more aggressive in its defence, making the task harder, until exhaustion set in. This baiting or drawing of the badger was really nothing more than worrying the badger in a confined space with no escape.

Rules for organised dog fighting would, no doubt, have varied according to the area of the Country and, perhaps, the whims of the owners but the basic rules were that fights were divided into rounds. Dogs were "tasted" at the start of the fight by an official paid to undertake the task of running his tongue all over each dog to ensure that no substance had been put on the dogs coat to put off its opponent. A thick line ("the scratch") was drawn in the centre and at each round one of the dogs in turn had to cross the scratch. If a dog failed to cross the scratch either through exhaustion, injury or lack of pluck, it was disqualified. An owner who saw that his dog was being beaten could "turn it in" (withdraw it) and forfeit his money. I think that many a good dog would have suffered by its owner not wishing such a forfeit.

The following is a description of a dog fighting and bear baiting den from 1828 at the Green Dragon Yard, Holborn, London, for which we are indebted to the London Evening Standard for the descriptive narrative:

> *This Pit, as it is called, is a loft about 25 feet square, with a fireplace and in one corner of the apartment is a space enclosed with green baize, where the proprietor, his wife and children sleep and eat. Two bears, several dogs, foxes and badgers are chained to the wall all around, many of which are in cages heaped upon each other.*
>
> *The centre is enclosed with boards about three feet high, containing an area of about eight feet square, where the dogs fight and bears and badgers are baited. On entering this elegant amphitheatre, the smell, as may be well*

supposed, is almost offensive and the noise of the dogs, bears and rabble most appalling and forming a nuisance to the whole neighbourhood.

The company consist of butchers, brickmakers and others, who do not appear to live by honest industry. These are the fellows who mostly bring the dogs. About an hour and a half is spent in dog fighting, then the bear is brought forward and fastened to a ring in the centre of the pit, with a chain about two feet in length, when one dog at a time is slipped at him. In one case, the bear being very young was much lacerated by several fierce bulldogs and bled profusely but still evinced, though unmuzzled, the utmost docility and good nature, holding up his bleeding paw as if to reproach his cruel master. He was led in and out by a little boy who, at the intervals of torture, rode on his back.

The whole concludes with a badger bait. The animal is confined in a long cage and a door at one end being opened and one dog at a time is slipped. The greatest cruelty occurs when what are called matches take place, the dogs frequently fighting till one or both are killed.

Dog fighting became illegal in 1835 but was definitely openly continued long after that date. The law did not either appear to be obeyed by the participants of the sport or enforced by the authorities. Challenges for dog fights and reports of dog fights appeared each week in the Canine columns of the press, with the location of the dog fight and the participants being clearly named: The Era, 31st October 1847 *The match between Peter Crawley's dog Cribb and Jemmy Shaw's dog Butcher for 5 sovs* (sovereigns) *a side came off on Thursday morning when, after a good fight of nearly one hours duration, Butcher was decided the winner;* The Era, 5th December 1847 *Mr Smith's white bitch of Handsworth and Blind Robert's red and white bitch of Wednesbury, fought for 5 sovs a side on Monday morning, each bitch weighing six and twenty pounds. The betting was 5 to 4 on Smith's. The fight lasted twenty minutes, the battle going in favour of the red and white, in consequence of the other refusing to scratch.* The Era edition on 13th February 1848, whilst noting that *the great match for 25 sovs aside between Mr W Jones's celebrated red and white dog, Toss from Oldbury and Mr Wilkins's black and white dog, Pilot, 29lbs each dog, was stopped by two inspectors of the Police. They fought above an hour and on being parted were much exhausted. We have since heard that Toss is dead.* The report does not say whether the participants were arrested and then the report goes on, nonchalantly: *The other matches of the week we sum up as follows: J Hawes red and white bitch, Nell, against E Reeves's Sheffield bitch Nettle, 5 sovs aside, 23lbs; 2 and 3 to 1 on Nell, who lost in 55 minutes, by refusing to scratch, she died directly. Bradley's brindled from Willenhall and T Fowler's Wolverhampton brindled dog, 5 sovs aside, 29lbs, ended in 25 minutes by the defeat of the former dog. Jem Parker's white dog Spot and Joseph Pritchard's brindled dog Tyrant, 5 sovs aside, 17lbs weight, three quarters of an hour witnessed the victory of Parker's dog – three scratches. Ben Terry's brindled bitch, Puss and T Clewley's black and white dog, Billy, 5 sovs aside, 17lbs, although chiefly in Billy's favour, he turned up a coward and refused to scratch in five and forty minutes.*

It was not until the early 1850's that participants really started to be charged for assisting and abetting in dog fights but that did not stop the open organisation of dog fights, which were reported in the press in the mid to late 1850's, for example, the Manchester Examiner reports that in Blackburn, October 1855, five Constables of the Police where desperately wounded when they tried to stop a dog fight near Myton Church. The crowd of over 150 spectators turned on them *in a most ferocious manner. The names of several are known and warrants have been issued for their apprehension.* This attack on the police may well have been the point at which the authorities decided that a real crackdown on public dog fighting was in order. Dog fighting continued but went underground, only available to those *in the know.*

The Birmingham Journal reported on a proposed dog fight at a pub in Manchester Street, Birmingham as late as March 1859. The event coming to light because one of the fights did not come off and Mr Smith took Mr Parsons to Court for the return of his stake money. *The learned Judge held, as he does in these and wager cases, that the matter was an illegal one and gave the plaintiff the verdict.* On 4th February 1860, the Staffordshire Sentinel reported that a dog fight involving a dozen persons had been stopped at a house in Hanley. The perpetrators being committed for a month to the House of Correction.

Ratting was a great sport practised in many pubs and back street arenas nationwide. One of the most famous being the Westminster Pit. The Westminster Pit really hosted contests of dogs against any animal that could stand against them, together with dog fighting and rat killing matches, badger and bear baiting. It was here that "Billy" a cross bred bulldog became a rat killing phenomenon, not only that but Billy was said to also mill well with dogs, draw the badger and serve out the bear.

However, so good was Billy at rat killing (that meaning, no doubt, that it was the best wager winner) that he was retired from these other pursuits. Billy was bred and owned by Charley Aistrop, who sold him as a pup to a gentleman called Charlie Drew and then, around 1810, paid some fifty guineas to buy him back. However, Billy's record did not last and the World record for rat killing was made in London in the early 1860's by a dog, called Jacko, a three quarter terrier and one quarter Bulldog weighing 13lbs, whose recorded feats were stunning: 25 rats killed in 1 minute 28 seconds on 20th August 1861; 100 rats killed in 5 minutes 28 seconds on 1st May 1862; and 1000 rats killed in 100 minutes on 1st May 1862. The thousand rats were not, of course, all killed in one event. The thousand rats were the culmination of ten separately timed events. For example, Bells Life in London and Sporting Chronicle" ("Bells Life") reported on the seventh on the 13th April 1862:

> *Did Jacko again successful destroying the seventh 100 rats in extraordinary style last Tuesday evening, in the presence of a numerous and highly respectable company at Jemmy Shaw's old favourite repost, Queen's Head Tavern, Crown Court, Windmill Street, Haymarket. The eighth 100 rats to be in the pit next Tuesday evening at nine o'clock precisely. The sagacity*

and cunning style of this extraordinary little animal's destroying mind must be seen to be credited, previous to his being put on the shelf.

Jacko was owned by Jemmy Shaw who was one of the "sporting" raconteur's of the 1850's/1860's. Another "sporting" raconteur of that time was none other than Bill Tupper who is reviewed in further detail when covering the Puss fight.

There is no doubt that illegal dog fights would be held in the backyards and cellars of taverns but these would be most secretive events for those *in the know*. Count Hollender recounts in his book "The Bull Terrier and All About It" published in 1932 that, on one occasion, he and the Earl of Rothes were paid £20 to loan out two of their dogs for a period of forty eight hours. Unbeknown to Count Hollender, the dogs had been matched to fight. Count Hollender recounted that only one returned home: *Pity Me killed his own grandfather in a Bank Holiday fight for £50 a side, the fight having lasted for over two hours, both these dogs had killed badgers single handed previously.*

It may be that some readers feel that I have dwelled too long on these unsavoury subjects but I feel that it is important to inject a slice of factual realism as to the attitude and mind set of people in the early 1860's and also set the scene for the Puss fight at Bill Tupper's in Long Acre. Far from such a fight being out of the question in London in the early 1860's, Jemmy Shaw's son William, who took over the business at the Queen's Head Tavern, Great Windmill Street, Haymarket, London was summoned to appear before the Marlborough Street Police Court as late as December 1870 *for unlawfully keeping and acting in the management of a place for the purpose of fighting and baiting certain animals, namely dogs and rats.*

In view of the fact that in Victorian England, a quarter of the population was most probably living in poverty, it is interesting to note in particular the amounts of money being wagered and the prizes on offer. During the Victorian era, the middle class was growing and those who were better off could have at least one servant. The upper middle classes were made up of financiers and merchants whilst the lower middle class comprised of small manufacturers, shopkeepers, clerks, teachers and managerial officials. The Census at the time tells us that, in 1851, around 1% – 2 % of the population had an income of over £150 per year. Income and class were not directly related and it was possible for a middle class clerk to earn less than a working class cotton spinner. The clerk's elevation in social status was due to his manner, dress and background. Common labourers would earn roughly 3s. 9d per week and ones with a skill, such as a bricklayer double that.

Jemmy Shaw had been a featherweight champion boxer in the 1840's but was also involved throughout that time in various sporting drums. Reviewing Jemmy Shaw does help to set the scene of the pursuits of the sporting fraternity and, in particular, the mindset of general society, both high and low, towards these activities during the 1860's. Take these "Canine Fancy" plugs from November 1862, March and April 1863 issues of the sporting newspaper of the time, Bells Life in London:

> *The great dog show is fixed to take place at Shaw's, the Queen's Head, Windmill Street, Haymarket, on Tuesday evening, May 21, on which occasion all the best fanciers in London will attend and exhibit their studs of pets....*
>
> *Ratting sports at Jemmy Shaw's far famed sporting house, Queen's Head Tavern, Crown Court, Windmill Street, Haymarket. On Tuesday evening, March 3rd, the Great All England Ratting Sweepstakes for handsome prizes comes off at Shaw's. Plenty of sport will follow with large ferrets etc, there will be about 300 fresh barn rats for public and private sport, with every convenience at any hour, day or evening. Old Jacko out again, being matched for £10 a side against Mr B's famous dog to destroy 100 rats each, which comes off on Tuesday, March 17th and already causes great interest. The "Treatise on Rats" can be had of Jemmy Shaw for 12 postage stamps, sent free to any part to stamped address. Jemmy Shaw's miniature museum is now open on view, free to the public generally. Old Tiny, the original Little Wonder, also the famous pure bulldogs, Crib, Billy, Blanch, Rob Roy, Cheyne Eye, Old Jem, Jacko etc etc; also the massive handsome prizes, goblets, cups, collars, medals etc etc can be seen at the bar at any time free to all.*
>
> *The ratting sweepstakes, for handsome and valuable prizes, comes off at Shaw's sporting establishment, the Queen's Head, Tavern.......the first to take choice of a handsome gold watch or valuable silver collar; second best*

> *dog a solid silver medal or handsome goblet; third dog a slip and collar. Dogs can be entered till half past eight o'clock. Nearly all the best dogs in England are already entered. The celebrated Jacko will display.*

> *Billy and Jacko – the 100 rat match between Mr N's Billy and Jemmy Shaw's Jacko, for £10 a side, came off on Tuesday evening March 31, Jacko winning by three seconds, destroying all in 8min 46sec. A match was afterwards made between Billy and Mr Strugnell's Bounce to destroy 100 rats for £10 a side, on Tuesday next.*

Jemmy Shaw's interests also extended into other sports: *Grand sparring and wrestling exhibitions, galaxy and combinations on Saturday, Monday and Wednesday evening April 4, 6 and 8 and during the holidays at Jemmy Shaw's far famed and commodious arena, Queen's Head Tavern, Windmill Street, Haymarket, under the able management of the youthful Jemmy Shaw himself, assisted by the Young Champion William Shaw, and all the elite of the fancy, too numerous to mention, have faithfully promised to attend. The public sparring, as usual (established for over half a century) carried on with great spirit every Saturday and Monday evening, in a new commodious roped ring at Jemmy Shaw's, causes great interest; great preparations are made for the dog show and friendly lead on 12th April, entrance fee, open to all.*

At these sporting houses, shows of dogs would be held every couple of weeks at which well known breeders would be invited to show their dogs. There was a Chairman and Vice Chairman who were well known exhibitors and would bring their top dogs along for spectators to view. These regular shows of dogs gave the opportunity for their owners (quite often the landlords of the tavern hosting the event) and guests to show their dogs against others and provide a saleroom for studs and puppies and, of course, bring in a crowd who would spend at the bar.

Dog owners would also issue challenges through Bells Life to other owners, either to settle an argument or to promote their dog. Take these examples: *Mr Wilbrow will match a dog 32lb weight, that has only got one eye and one tooth, to destroy 100 or 200 rats, for £5 or £10 a side.* Mr Wilbrow was landlord of the King's Head, White Lion Street, London, which was one of many sporting drums in London in the 1850's and 1860's. *If Mr R..... really meant what he said at the Islington Dog Show, Mr F...... of Norwood will meet him at S*

Millard's Builders Arms, Boundary Street, Shoreditch, prepared to show a bull bitch under 12 months old against any of Mr R.....'s for any sum up to £25 a side.

We should also bear in mind that these "sporting" people and dog dealers were not common labourers earning 3s. 9d per week. £25 was a huge wager in those times. This clearly indicates that those involved in these sporting activities, including dog showing and dog dealing, were pretty well off for the times and would "mix" with those both high and low – as James Hinks did himself.

James Hinks both issued and was the recipient of challenges: take this one from the Birmingham Daily Post in September 1866: *James Hinks, 53 Worcester Street, will SHOW his Bull Dog "Romsey" AGAINST any Bull Dog or Bitch in Birmingham for £10 and will leave the same to any competent judge in the town.* Following the Birmingham Show in 1860, at which James Hinks exhibited and won first prize in the Bulldog class, two such challenges were issued in the Sporting Life to him. These intriguing and very telling challenges, together with other contemporary evidence from 1860, will be considered further when reviewing the fable of Old Madman "the Bulldog."

The New Bulldog

The Bulldog had been in decline for very many years and, when you consider the uses to which it was put for so many generations and the type of people that owned them, this was not surprising. However, dog shows were to be the saviour of the National breed, starting with shows of dogs week in week out in Inns and sporting houses in the 1840's and 1850's and then to larger organised dog shows in the 1860's, albeit that the up to date show bench bulldogs began to bear less and less resemblance to their more active and ferocious forebears. Having said that, there were certain sections who wished to recreate the bulldog of old and others who did not wish to lose the basic Bulldog characteristics. Jemmy Shaw, for example, regularly hosted shows of *Old Time Bulldogs.*

Bill George emphasised this change in attitude. Bill George started life as a butcher's boy and progressed into being a bare knuckle prize fighter, he then became an apprentice of Ben White of Kensal New Town, London who was one of the old time dog dealers, engaged in dog fighting, ratting, badgering and cock fighting, in fact anything that his young gentlemen patrons may desire for their amusement. Ben White died in the same year that Bull baiting was outlawed and Bill George bought the premises from his widow, changing its name to "Canine Castle" whereupon it became known as a relative centre of respectability dealing in show dogs, particularly Bulldogs.

Around 1840, Bill George imported a Spanish Bulldog whom he named Big Headed Billy to help in his creation of a Bulldog line that retained the characteristics of the breed but more amenable. This gave rise to Bill George's famous Dan who was a grandson of Big Headed Billy. Others, such as Frank Adcock imported Spanish Bulldogs to interbreed with their English stock. Adcock's Toro (later owned by Mr Dawes) was said to weigh 90lbs and its sire and dam were both purebred Spanish Bulldogs weighing over 90lbs. James Hinks, himself, imported a cropped bulldog called Crib, born in 1869, sired by a French Bordelais Bulldog out of a litter sister of Lamphier's King Dick, which he then exhibited and mated to some of his English Bulldog stock.

Bill George's reputation was such that, in October 1863, he received a visit from the Prince Napoleon, as reported in Bells Life: *The object of Prince Napoleon in visiting this Country was to have an interview with him on the subject of dog shows and other important matters. His imperial highness was received by William George on Monday last at Canine Castle, Kensal New Town and conducted over the establishment with which he was much pleased. He had the gratification of joining in the noble sport of hunting that ferocious animal, the British rat – a chasse of which was got up for his amusement. The Prince afterwards purchased some of William's beauties, left substantial tokens of his pleasure with George jun; and having obtained a model of William's best hat for his own adoption, took his departure with his suite.* Napoleon certainly had an interest in dog shows as he exhibited at the first French Dog Show in May 1863 where, not surprisingly, his Foxhounds won first prize. The French show will be further reviewed in a later chapter.

It is not surprising that arguments and challenges took place over bulldogs because there were generally three different types of bulldog being promoted, ranging in weight from around 6lb to over 60lbs. One type would, in the end win through, though that is a bulldog story told in many bulldog breed history books. The relevance for bull terriers is that James Hinks's bulldogs, in particular exhibited at Birmingham in 1860 and 1861 and at Holborn in 1862, appear to have been the subject of much discussion and disagreement amongst bulldog fanciers – including Bill Tupper.

The favoured colours for bulldogs, as described by F T Barton in The Kennel Encyclopaedia were *whole or "smut" (that is, a whole colour with a black mask or muzzle).* This is confirmed by Idstone, who related that the preferred colours for a bulldog were whole unmixed colours and white bulldogs were preferred by many. After pure white, white Bulldogs with a black muzzle were next in line, such dogs being described as a white "smut". Next in order of colour merit was clear red or red smut, then fawn or fawn smut. After these, Idstone then had his own preference towards the brindled Bulldog and also favoured a white with a few brindle marks, especially one with brindle cheeks and ears with a white blaze down the face. Idstone alluded that, on a white dog, *marks on one side are more objectionable than a spot at the root of the tail.* Those latter comments on the Bulldog still hold true for the Bull Terrier some 140 odd years later. Again, Idstone's remarks on the head of the Bulldog also still hold true for the Bull Terrier of today; *The head of the Bulldog is all important and no dog with an indifferent or second rate head can make up for it by large bones or excellence of coat or colour.*

Bells Life reported on regular shows of Bulldogs being held at sporting establishments in London throughout the 1850's, one of the staunch Bulldog men was Mr James Ferriman. Mr Ferriman was one of the London school of "old doggy men" and was Landlord of the Graham Arms, City Road, London, which was another of the London sporting drums. Mr Ferriman also specialised in small size bull terriers for use in ratting contests. Dogs and ferrets were not the only animals used by Mr Ferriman, he had a rat destroying badger on view and also a mongoose in action.

The Kennel Club was founded in April 1873. One of the founders being Mr S E Shirley, who was a keen exhibitor of several breeds, particularly Bull Terriers. The first KC Stud Book covering the period 1859 to 1873 was not compiled until 1874, making this a mammoth task in the collection of reliable information which, in the main, had to come from breeders and owners. The KC applied to owners for details of over 3500 pedigrees but many letters were either unanswered or returned marked "gone away". For the accuracy of some information and certainly for the notes that accompanied some of the Bulldog details and some of the Bull Terrier details, we are indebted to Mr Adcock who reviewed the Bulldogs and Mr Shirley who reviewed the Bull Terriers. Not all winning dogs from the early shows were included, particularly for a new breed like the Bull Terrier, where classes were only just being provided.

Whilst the early pedigrees of Bull Terriers were quite often either sparse or suspect, those of the Bulldog were generally, with exceptions, somewhat more reliable. It is possible to trace the pedigrees of the leading Bulldogs of the day back through very many generations. Bill George, for example, claimed to know the pedigree of his bulldog Crib going back some fifty years.

The Fable of Old Madman "the Bulldog"

Old Madman "the Bulldog" is one of the great foundation stories in the breed's history and, after thorough investigation, it turns out to be wholly false.

Let's start with Old Madman "the Bulldog's" claim to fame. That he was exhibited in the Bulldog class at the Birmingham Show in December 1860, won the class and was said to be sired by Jim Ward's Crib out of Smut.

Contemporary evidence overwhelmingly proves that this claim to fame is wholly untrue. The pedigree of Old Madman "the Bulldog" is based purely on the untrue tale and must, therefore, also be incorrect.

The verifiable contemporary evidence from the 1860's, which includes the judges critique of the bulldog class at the Birmingham Show, clearly shows that a great inaccuracy has been perpetuated by the conformists over the last 160 years, simply rewriting and, in some cases, even embellishing the fiction and fable that had been written before. Having been historically misled for nearly 160 years, I believe that breed enthusiasts should know the facts, so I will not beat about the bush:

OLD MADMAN "THE BULLDOG" WAS NOT SHOWN AT BIRMINGHAM IN 1860. HINKS'S WINNING BULLDOG AT THE 1860 BIRMINGHAM SHOW WAS A WHITE BITCH. OLD MADMAN WAS OF PEDIGREE UNKNOWN, PROBABLY A BULL TERRIER.

On Monday and Tuesday, 3rd and 4th December 1860, The National Exhibition of sporting and other dogs was held at Midland Counties Repository, Cheapside in Birmingham. Only one prize per breed was offered. The winning dogs at the show were not named, only the name of the owner/exhibitor was given. There was a class for Bulldogs with five entries with James Hinks indeed winning the class.

The report of the Birmingham show in the Birmingham Journal, again, does not give either the name or sex of the winning Bulldog but it does state the breeding: *the first prize being taken by a white animal the property of Mr James Hinks, of Birmingham, by Jim Ward's "Crib" out of "Smut".*

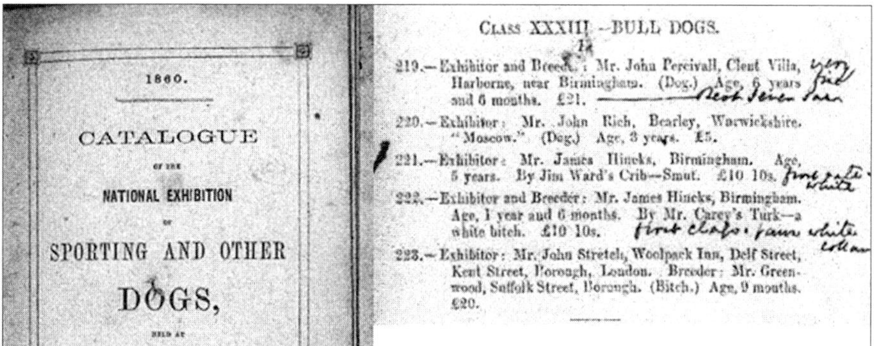

1860.

CATALOGUE OF THE NATIONAL EXHIBITION OF SPORTING AND OTHER DOGS, HELD AT The Midland Counties Repository, CHEAPSIDE, BIRMINGHAM, ON MONDAY & TUESDAY, DECEMBER 3RD & 4TH.

BIRMINGHAM: PRINTED BY M. BILLING, LIVERY STREET.

CLASS XXXIII.—BULL DOGS.

219.—Exhibitor and Breeder: Mr. John Percivall, Cleut Villa, Harborne, near Birmingham. (Dog.) Age, 6 years and 6 months. £21.

220.—Exhibitor: Mr. John Rich, Bearley, Warwickshire. "Moscow." (Dog.) Age, 3 years. £5.

221.—Exhibitor: Mr. James Hincks, Birmingham. Age, 5 years. By Jim Ward's Crib—Smut. £10 10s.

222.—Exhibitor and Breeder: Mr. James Hincks, Birmingham. Age, 1 year and 6 months. By Mr. Carey's Turk—a white bitch. £10 10s.

223.—Exhibitor: Mr. John Stretch, Woolpack Inn, Delf Street, Kent Street, Borough, London. Breeder: Mr. Greenwood, Suffolk Street, Borough. (Bitch.) Age, 9 months. £20.

The unknown spectator to whom the catalogue belonged made his own notes :
219 Exhibitor, John Percival - "Very fine, best I ever saw"
221 Exhibitor James Hinks - "first rate white"
222 Exhibitor James Hinks - "first class, fawn white collar"

The Bells Life reporter confirmed the details: *While Mr Hincks' prize "bull"..... maintained the varmint character of appearance by quite as orthodox a pedigree – by Jim Ward's Crib out of Smut. The two red bulldogs were by no means of so fine a stamp.* One of the red bulldogs referred to was also exhibited and bred by Hinks. Again, neither the name of this bulldog or its sex was stated in the catalogue but it was given to be 1 year and six months old, sired by *Carey's Turk* out of *a white bitch.*

Idstone, whose book "The Dog" was published in 1872, described the winning Bulldog in question and I believe that Idstone's description became the source of 160 years of historical error: *One of the first Bulldogs exhibited which was worthy of the name belonged to Mr James Hinks of Birmingham. He was a white dog and gained the first prize in Mr Hinks's native town in 1860.* However, Idstone does not name the bulldog in question, nor its breeding, but he does refer to it as *a white dog*. The general term "bulldog" would certainly suggest a dog. In Idestone's book did he, perhaps, take his description of Old Madman "the Bulldog" from a newspaper report of a later show in 1862 at which Hinks's bulldog bitch (called "Madman" and sired by Jim Ward's Crib) won her class: *the truest type of the Bull species that we have seen for some time (The Era,).*

So began the confusion and the fable that the animal winning the Bulldog class at Birmingham was (Old) Madman (sired by Jim Ward's Crib out of Smut) was born and the inaccuracy perpetuated and embellished by the conformists.

There was already heated debate about what a good bulldog should look like and this was the case with Hinks's bitch at Birmingham. The Judges report and other comments on Hinks's winning bulldog bitch at Birmingham clearly indicate that views were strongly held, one aggrieved Brummie going as far as saying that Hinks's winning bulldog bitch contained much more terrier in her than bull!

Following the Birmingham Show on Monday and Tuesday, 3rd and 4th December 1860, two challenges were issued to James Hinks in Saturday, 8th December's issue of Sporting Life from people who apparently did attend the Birmingham show: *George Mosley, Prince of Wales Inn, Sheffield, will show a bull bitch against Mr J Hincks's bull bitch which obtained the first prize at Birmingham Show on Monday last for £5 or £10. A practical judge in London or Birmingham to decide. By sending money for a match to the Swan Inn, Upper Priory, or to this paper, Mr Hincks can be on.*

The second challenge was made by Mr Nightingale, Landlord of the Swann Inn who also happened to be the Sporting Life correspondent for the Birmingham and District area. Mr Nightingale clearly thought that John Percival's dog should have been placed over Hinks's bitch: *Mr Nightingale, Swan Inn, Birmingham, being surprised at the white bitch which got the first prize at the Birmingham Show being thus placed, will show the dog next to the bitch, if the owner will produce him, for £5, £10, or £20. Any competent judge in Birmingham or London to decide.*

The Judge at Birmingham was none other than the editor of The Field, the eminent J H Walsh (Stonehenge) and Walsh's own critique in Saturday, 15th

December 1860 issue of Illustrated London News emphasised why feelings were running a little high about Hinks's winning bulldog bitch: *The bulldogs were equally defective – the white bitch which obtained the prize being on the whole the best, but still very inferior in all points but tail to one of her competitors, which was deficient in this respect, having a very screw tail, hardly two inches long.*

Hinks's win with his bulldog bitch also prompted a letter to Bells Life from a very disgruntled Brummie: *Mr Editor: That our dog show was a great success must, I think, be a source of satisfaction to all lovers of that faithful and sagacious animal. This success, however, to the fancier was somewhat marred by the decisions of the judge in the classes "Dogs not used in field sports", more especially in the "Bulldog" and "Terrier" classes. The prize for Bulldogs was awarded to a sharp nosed, flat skulled, terrier bodied bitch, whilst the prize for "White and other English terriers" was awarded to a very pretty dog, showing what fanciers term a deal of breed or, in other words, a good deal of Bulldog. How the decisions in the two classes can be justified is above my comprehension........... I have an Italian Greyhound with a much finer tail than this white bitch, but had I sent it, it would have been no more entitled to a prize, as a Bulldog, than this half bred bull terrier bitch – Yours, &c, Old England – Birmingham, Dec 8.*

The renowned bulldog man, Bill George, even became embroiled in the controversy seeking clarification with a letter to the Editor of the other sporting newspaper of the time, Sporting Life: *Sir, – having been prevented by illness from attending the late dog show at Birmingham, I should esteem it a high favour if you will in your valuable and truthful paper inform me which of the two parties is right and which is wrong – the artist who drew the portraits of Mr James Hinckes's bulldog and Mr Wilkinson's toy terrier in the Illustrated London News or the penman behind the signature of "Old England" in Bells Life in London" The picture makes "the bull" to have a good round head and "the terrier" a sharp one. The latter asserts precisely the contrary and says (meaning I conclude to be witty) that the judge gave the prize to the dog with the best tail, which said tail ("stern" we call it) is not equal to that of his (wife's) Italian Greyhound.* The Editor replied: *We have always believed the artist of the Illustrated London News to give faithful delineations. They are, we believe, taken from photographs and we are therefore bound to consider them exact likenesses.*

A reproduction of the cover of Illustrated London News, Saturday, 15th December 1860, showing the artists depiction of Hinks's winning bulldog bitch is shown below. The depiction certainly appears to be a feminine bulldog bitch, so we should be able to discount "Old England's" disparaging remarks as sour grapes (perhaps he just did not like Walsh). We must also discount any possibility that Old Madman "the Bulldog" was either entered or won the bulldog class at this show.

For completeness the full cover page from the Saturday, 15th December 1860 issue of Illustrated London News giving the results of the 1860 Birmingham show is reproduced for the benefit of readers.

So, there we have it. The winning bulldog at the Birmingham Show in December 1860 was most definitely not Old Madman "the Bulldog" – but one of Hinks's white bulldog bitches, sired by *Jim Ward's Crib – Smut.* The name "Smut" would indicate that the mother was a white bitch with a black mask.

So, where does this leave Old Madman "the Bulldog". There is no doubt that a dog called Old Madman was mated to the iconic Puss, producing the famous bull terrier, also named Madman (born in 1862). There can also be no doubt now that the Old Madman put on Puss was clearly not the bulldog that won the class at the Birmingham Show in 1860, because the winner of that class was a bitch. In 1860 Hinks upped his game in bulldogs buying in a few related pedigree bulldogs from recognised breeders for line breeding and showing. However, whilst Hinks was happy to put Old Madman on his bull terriers, there is no contemporary evidence whatsoever that he mated Old Madman to any of the new line of pedigree bulldog bitches that he had bought in for exhibiting and breeding.

This raises the question whether Old Madman was a bulldog or, in fact, a bull terrier. James Jr asserted that his father *commenced to try and establish his new type of bull terrier in the 1850's and that this took some time.* This statement would appear correct, because there is clear evidence that James Hinks was breeding bull terriers in the mid 1850's, for example the stated pedigree of Puss (born in 1860) goes back some three generations to the mid/late 1850's. He also bred a bull terrier called "Spring" in 1857 (by Jerry ex Daisy) which again confirms that his bull terrier breeding programme started well before 1860 and, as we now know from the Birmingham show catalogue, Hinks's unnamed winning bulldog bitch at Birmingham in 1860 was born in 1855.

The further evidence that Old Madman was probably a bull terrier and not a bulldog is that the iconic Puss, her son the famous Madman, his litter brother (Roberts Madman) together with two other of his other bull terriers, Turk and Daisy, were stated in 1864 to be bred "true for type". Take this report from Bells Life of the show at Alexandra Park in 1864 as evidence that type had been established: *These are all white terriers of the same character, neat, short dogs, with a peculiar long head which, with the close cropped ears, gave them rather a vulgar than a handsome look.* Type could not have been established so soon if they were the product of a pure bred bulldog crossed with a half bred terrier.

So all the indications are that Old Madman was not a bulldog but a bull terrier "of pedigree unknown". Further contemporary evidence for this comes, perhaps, from the most meticulous Mr E E M Royds, who owned the famous Madman's other litter brother (known as Royds Madman). In the catalogue for the sixth Birmingham Show in 1865, Mr Royds gave detailed breeding of his Madman: *613.- Exhibitor: Mr E E M Royds, Greenhill, Rochdale, Lancashire. Breeder: Mr J Hinks. "Madman." Age, 3 years. By Old Madman-Old Puss. Old Puss by Rebel-Wasp. Rebel by Nip-Old Daisy. Wasp by Bustle-Fly. Fly by Salisbury's Nothing-Bob Elson's Nell. £100,000.* If the breeding behind Old Madman was known, the meticulous Mr Royds would have surely stated it. The first KC Stud Book also gives details of the pedigree of Hink's famous bull terrier Madman, again, there are no details stated of the breeding behind its sire, Old Madman, clearly indicating that Old Madman was "of pedigree unknown".

THE ILLUSTRATED LONDON NEWS.

No. 1064.—VOL. XXXVII.] SATURDAY, DECEMBER 15, 1860. [WITH A SUPPLEMENT, FIVEPENCE

INDIAN TAXATION.

"HAPPY is the country that has no history," says the proverbial philosopher. If there be any nation on the globe that is, or has been, entitled to enter into this charmed category, at least it cannot be British India. There have been occasionally times when the recurrent arrival of the mails have failed to create that temporary and spasmodic interest which it is to be feared is alone excited in the minds of the English public in regard to that country; but those times have been few, and generally far between. Indeed, those periods of tranquillity and absence of exciting intelligence have usually borne the character of that lull which in nature precedes the tempest. We have had enough, and to spare, of tidings of wars waged for the acquisition and the defence of territory, the necessary products of a policy which in a great empire is supposed to be that of glorious and

1. Lieutenant-Colonel Inge's Deerhound "Brimstone." 2. Mr. Jennings' Bloodhound. 3. Mr. Edgar Hanbury's Mastiff. 4. Lieutenant-Colonel Aikin's Newfoundland. 5. Mr. Henry Gilbert's small Pointer "Bob." 6. Mr. James Hincks's Bulldog. 7. Mr. Wilkinson's Toy Terrier (weight 3½ lb.). 8. Mr. J. Stretch's Maltese Lion Dog (weight 5lb.). 9. Mr. J. Stretch's King Charles's Spaniel.

NATIONAL EXHIBITION OF DOGS AT BIRMINGHAM.—SEE SUPPLEMENT, PAGE [illegible].

National Exhibition of Dogs at Birmingham. 6. Mr James Hincks's Bulldog

James Hinks

James Hinks was an obvious 19th century entrepreneur, looking for opportunities to improve his family's wellbeing. He found it in animals, selling breeding and dealing, birds, rabbits and various breeds of dogs. The dogs having the highest value and, therefore, worthy of concentration. Whilst there does not appear to be any indication that Hinks was involved in the promotion or participation in dog fighting, doing business with dog stealers was another matter. We should remember though that this was Birmingham in the mid 1800's and life was very different than today.

James Hinks married Elizabeth Moore in 1851, at the age of 22. It appears that Elizabeth, already had a son and a daughter from a previous relationship. These children, aged 4 and 2, were called John and Ann Bosworth who, after the marriage to Elizabeth, became known as John and Ann Hinks. In the Census for 1851, James Hinks is described as "Head" (of the household) and John Bosworth is described as "son". I do not read too much into this, as Ann Bosworth is described as "lass". The family lived in Coventry Street, St Martins, Birmingham. James Hinks was the head of the household and his occupation was that of a "Poulterer". The household also included a 15 year old Irish girl, called Ann Quenn, who was described as a "Servant". Over the next 10 years Elizabeth Hinks was to give birth to 6 children, the ones of note in the history of the Bull Terrier being the eldest, James Jr, born in 1851 and

Frederick (let's call him "Fred") born on 21st February 1853. By 1861 James Hinks's occupation was that of a "General Dealer" and the family lived in Philip Street, St Martins, Birmingham.

The Census records that in 1871, the family lived at 53 Worcester Street, St Martins, Birmingham, whilst Fred, aged 17, who was a clerk and Alfred, aged 15, described as a scholar, remained in the household, John, who was a cabinet case maker and James Jr, who was now a poultry dealer, were both in lodgings with a Mrs Sharp in Lower Hurst Street, St Martins.

It looks like Elizabeth Hinks may have had a preference for cats, as she took prizes for her long haired cat at the First National Cat Show held in Birmingham in 1873. She repeated this performance at the Second Cat Show the following year. Elizabeth Hinks died in her sleep on 5th May 1889.

James Hinks died on 23rd May 1878, of tuberculosis, at the age of 49. At that time he was described in official documents as a "General Dealer". The obituary in the Birmingham Daily Post was simple and loving:........ *James Hinks, of Worcester Street, this town; deeply lamented by his sorrowing wife, family and friends. His end was peace.......*

Hinks was said to be a very poor record keeper. I have never personally believed this to be correct as he appeared to be a most clever personality. He was a registered general dealer and keeping records of various sorts would form part of his business. This was confirmed to me by Tom Horner who told me told me that Hinks did keep records but a future relative destroyed them, not realising their importance. I do not know where Tom came by this information but I have no reason to doubt what he told me.

The Hinks's had several brushes with the law and, more often than not, came away smelling of roses usually through lack of evidence and, in one of the Court case involving James Hinks in early 1870, by a legal technicality. In 1874, it was Mrs Hinks potentially in the frame for receipt of stolen goods: *EXTENSIVE ROBBERIES FROM DRAPERS – William Raljohns (18) under warehouseman for Messrs Turner, Son and Nephew, drapers, New Street, was charged on remand with stealing silks, a rug, shawls, a velvet jacket, linen etc, value £30, belonging to his employers. Mr Buller appeared to prosecute. The prisoner had been in the employ of Messrs Turner about six months, during the whole of which time, it was alleged, he had been robbing his masters. The robbery being detected, the Police were communicated with – Detective Sergeant Seal said "from information received" went to the house of Mr Hinks, beerhouse keeper, Worcester Street, where he found the whole of the stolen property. The prisoner, it appeared, had been paying his addresses to Miss Hinks and had been very generous at his master's expense, for he had presented Miss Hinks with two dresses, two shawls, a velvet jacket, several hankerchiefs etc. The remaining part of the stolen goods were sold to Mrs Hinks. The prisoner pleaded guilty and was sentenced to six months hard labour. Mr Parry, who appeared to watch the case on behalf of Mrs Hinks, said the prisoner was looked upon by the Hinks's as an honourable young man and they had no knowledge of the things having been stolen. Upon application of Mr Buller, the Magistrate directed that the goods recovered be given up to Messrs Turner.*

So, what of the dogs! James Hinks, using his credentials as a registered trader, also added dog dealing to his craft. The new dog shows provided him with an outlet for his entrepreneurial skills. He became a keen exhibitor, the new dog shows being a great market place for selling his stock of various breeds to the gentry. He bred, exhibited and dealt in many breeds, although the ones of main concern to us are the Bulldog, English White Terrier, Dalmatian, Greyhound and, of course, the Bull Terrier. The first Kennel Club Stud Book in 1874, covering the early shows from 1859 to 1873 discloses that James Hinks had Stud Book entries for all five breeds, some of the dogs were home bred and others, like the Greyhound, were bought in.

It has often been written that James Hinks would not have had much space in the yard of his house or Inn in which to keep many dogs. That may have been so when he was residing in Philip Street. However, when he moved to 53 Worcester Street, he clearly believed that the premises afforded ample space for his dog and bird dealing activities, as advertised in Bells Life on 9th September 1865: *BIRMINGHAM REPOSITORY for DOGS and BIRDS – J Hinks wishes to inform the public that he has REMOVED from his late premises in Philip Street and has now opened his more commodious premises, 53 Worcester Street, close to the Market Hall and Railway Station, where they will find a splendid collection of dogs of all breeds, with fancy and foreign birds for sale.*

We have a very good description of the size of 53 Worcester Street from a licensing application made by James Hinks in August 1868: *Four spare bedrooms, club room 37 feet by 14 feet, stabling for three horses, house rented at £80 and rated at £45 per year.*

Also, in the 1860's, a dog dealers stock appeared only to be limited by the length of the chains upon which they were kept. James Watson, author of The Dog Book, published in 1906, describes a visit with his father to Bill George's respectable "Canine Castle" in London: *It was with fear and trembling we crept along between the rows of furiously barking and chain tugging dogs.* Watson also notes that Bill George's Bulldogs *were mainly white with patches of colour.* There is a Punch cartoon of a visit to Bill George's Canine Castle which supports James Watson's description of how the dogs were kept. This is further confirmed by an 1860's article in Bells Life: *In a large yard at the back of what we must still by courtesy call the castle were the dogs – dogs in truth of every known kind and description, in good condition and tolerably clean. Such of the animals as were in kennels had a neat semi circle patch of straw in front of their abodes on which they stood when called out for inspection....we were shown about half a dozen of the most beautiful bulldogs it ever was my lot to see.* An advert from Bill George in The Sporting Life, 25th June 1862, claimed that there were upwards of 250 dogs of all breeds for sale at his premises. Contemporary evidence suggests that James Hinks kept around 60 dogs at 53 Worcester Street.

In 1858, James Hinks bought a bulldog bitch called "Pet" from the noted London breeder Mr James Ferriman and, in 1860, he really upped his game, buying in from Jack Holland, a Birmingham Bulldog breeder, a bitch puppy, which he named "Madman" [2690] by Ward's Cribb out of Holland's Poll. The Catalogue of the second Birmingham Show in 1861 contains a printing error and calls the bitch "Wadman", however James Hinks showed this bulldog bitch a few times always under the name of "Madman" and that is verified by the entry for the 1861 Birmingham show in the first Kennel Club Stud Book. We can see an extended pedigree for James Hinks's first Bulldog entry into the KC Stud Book, that being Hinks's bulldog bitch, "Madman" said to be born around August 1860. Many thanks to Bill Lambert and Ciara Farrell at the KC Library for their help in this respect, as the copy of the KC Stud Book for 1874, which I had downloaded from the Archive.org website, had a page missing, which Ciara kindly supplied.

<table>
<tr><td rowspan="8">Hinks's
Bulldog Bitch

MADMAN

Born around
August 1860.
KC Stud Book
2690</td><td rowspan="4">Ward's Crib</td><td rowspan="2">Percival's Toss</td><td>Percival's Old Nick</td></tr>
<tr><td>Harry Edmonds Venny</td></tr>
<tr><td rowspan="2">Ned Davis's Luce</td><td>Tailby's Tumbler</td></tr>
<tr><td>Smith's Pat</td></tr>
<tr><td rowspan="4">Holland's Poll</td><td rowspan="2">Carey's Charlie</td><td>Percival's Toss</td></tr>
<tr><td>His Duchess</td></tr>
<tr><td rowspan="2">Smith's Pat</td><td>Tailby's Tumbler</td></tr>
<tr><td>Tailby's Lady</td></tr>
</table>

Hinks also bought in a bitch puppy from an old time Bulldog breeder, Joseph Carey, which he named "Rose" [2709] by Carey's Charlie out of Carey's Nettle. Holland's Poll was also sired by Carey's Charlie, so did James Hinks have an eye on line breeding his Bulldogs? He then bought in a dog from Jack Holland called Nelson [2637] sired by the top Bulldog of the day, Lamphier's King Dick and the dam was, again, Holland's Poll. At the Leeds show in July 1861, the winning bitch, owned by Mr Fearn, was called Rush [2711] by Lillian's

Spring out of Lillian's Nettle (Spring by Gambler out of Nuttal's brindle pied bitch, Gambler was by Burke's Crib, Nettle was by Davis's Wasp). Mr Fearn also showed Rush at the Second Birmingham Show in December 1861 and James Hinks wasted little time in buying this winning bitch from Mr Fearn to add to his growing kennel of pedigree Bulldogs. A few years later, he was to sell Rush to a Mr Whitehouse whereupon, at the age of 6, she again became a first prize winner.

The conformists say that Hinks gave up on bulldogs because he could not beat Lamphier's dog, King Dick. However, this is not so. There is no doubt that James Hinks's love of the bulldog remained throughout his life as he continued to show and breed them. Even in 1870, when the conformists mistakenly say that Hinks stopped showing, he showed his bulldog Crib at Manchester in December of that year. The reasons for his exile from the show scene are reviewed in a subsequent chapter.

1861 was also the year in which James Hinks produced the iconic Puss. The date that Puss was born has been open to debate. The first KC Stud Book gives her date of birth as *about 1860*. Newspaper reports of shows are not able to provide any certainty to corroborate this date. A report in the 23rd April 1864 issue of Aris's Birmingham Gazette of the second Ashburnham Dog Show (Cremorne) held in April 1864, *Third prize, Mr James Hinks, Puss, aged 4 years.* That would give Puss's date of birth as around April 1860, corresponding with the KC Stud Book. However, eight months later, a report in the 3rd December 1864 issue of Birmingham Journal of The National Exhibition of sporting and other dogs held at the Old Wharf in Birmingham in early December 1864 reports *Second: exhibitor and breeder, Mr J Hinks, Phillip Street, Birmingham "Puss" age 3 years and 3 months.* This puts her being born around September 1861. If we look further for corroboration, we find that the Aris's report for the December 1865 Birmingham show reports: *Mr James Hinks, Puss, age 4 years, 3 months* and the Aris's report of the 1866 Birmingham show is also consistent, *2nd, exhibitor and breeder, Mr James Hinks, 53 Worcester Street "Old Puss" age 5 years 3 months.* These consistent reports of Puss's age give comfort that she was most probably born around September 1861.

The date of birth of Puss's son, the famous Bull Terrier Madman, is similarly confused, with the first KC Stud Book giving him as *born in 1862.*

Madman

Aris's Birmingham Gazette reporting on the second Ashburnham Dog Show (Cremorne) held in April 1864 reports: *First prize, breeding, Mr James Hinks, Birmingham, Madman age 1 year 7 months by Old Madman out of Old Puss,* putting him born in September 1862, whilst Aris's reports that the famous Madman's litter sister at the same show: *Second Prize, Mr James Hinks, Puss, aged 2 years,* putting the litter whelped in April 1862. The Birmingham Journal of 3rd December 1864, reporting on the Birmingham Show states that the famous Madman was *2 years* old, putting him born in December 1862. However, the same report gives his litter sister Puss, then in the ownership of Mr Walker, as being *2 years and 6 months* old, putting their whelping date as June 1862. Seeking corroboration from other reports, we find that Aris's report of the Birmingham show in December 1865 contains the details of the famous Madman's litter brother (known as Royds Madman): *Second, Mr E.E.M. Royds, Greenhill, Rochdale, "Madman" age 3 years.* This, again, provides some corroborative comfort that the correct date for Puss whelping the Madman litter was most probably December 1862.

The first KC Stud Book also gives details of the pedigree of Puss: *by Hinks's Rebel out of Wasp; Rebel by Nib out of Old Daisy; Wasp by Bustle out of Fly; Fly by Salisbury's Nothing out of Bob Elson's Nell.* Unfortunately, there are no details of the breeds represented by these names. However, on pure conjecture based on the fact that Hinks would use an individual name several times and using the KC Stud Book as a reference, we can say that Hinks appeared to separate names by their breed, for example, it appears that: he used "Rebel" for naming Bull Terriers; "Daisy" for Bull Terriers; "Wasp" for both Bull Terriers and Bulldogs; "Fly" for English White and other smooth coated terriers, together with a greyhound and none of these names appeared to be used by Hinks for naming Dalmatians. This, if it were so and I make no claims whatsoever that it is so, would give us Puss's sire, "Rebel", being a bull terrier and her mother "Wasp" either a bull terrier or a bulldog. Puss was said to be refined, which would indicate that her mother, "Wasp" would not be a bulldog. If "Fly" was a white smooth haired terrier, then "Bustle" would have been either a bulldog or a bull terrier, confirming "Wasp" to be a bull terrier rather than a bulldog.

This would give either one or both of Wasp's parents to also be a bull terrier. As we now know that Old Madman was most likely a bull terrier "of pedigree unknown" it follows that Hinks's bull terriers were commencing to breed "true to type" as evidenced by the report from Bells Life of the show at Alexandra Park in 1864: *These are all white terriers of the same character, neat, short dogs, with a peculiar long head.*

There is nothing particularly strange about interbreeding in the 1850's and 1860's as, with the advent of dog shows, first in "sporting drums" then larger organised shows, many breeds underwent alteration by judicious crosses with other breeds. The first KC Stud Book shows winning Bulldogs with terriers in their pedigree and White English Terriers/smooth haired terriers with bull terriers in their pedigree.

It has been said that Hinks's use of a Dalmatian in the creation of the bull terrier was genius. However, such a cross was certainly not a new idea. Such crosses between terrier type dogs and Dalmatians were noted in *The Sportsman's Repository* by the then author of British Field Sports, Lawrence John, published as far back as 1820. The terrier types would have been either solid for colour or black and tan, carrying little white and the resultant cross was known as the Harlequin: *It is said, a spotted variety of the terrier kind, marked with white, tan colour and black, has of late years been introduced to some parts of the Kingdom and as they have never been so numerous, they have been in proportioned high estimation and some have been sold at considerable prices. They are found to possess agreeable qualities, having all the spirit of sporting dogs, with the attachment of the most faithful of their kind, blended with all the elegance. We know not what breed this can be, unless one between the Coach Dog and Terrier, which we have experienced and of which the name, as given to us, was the Harlequin breed. We have found them most excellent vermin dogs and faithful keepers.* What was new was the use of white terriers with the Dalmatian with the intention of producing a white bull terrier, retaining the terrier spirit whilst improving bodylines.

There is circumstantial evidence that a surreptitious back cross with a Greyhound may have been introduced as a refinement over the next few years. A Greyhound owner mating his Greyhound to a Bulldog or Bull terrier to give his Greyhounds more bottle had been well established. We will consider whether James Hinks used a Greyhound or Greyhound cross as a back cross when reviewing Old Victor in a subsequent chapter.

It has been said that there may be Pointer blood behind the Bull Terrier and, certainly, some Bull Terriers will stand and point, even lifting one front leg off the ground whilst doing so. This does not mean that such blood was introduced by James Hinks, although he did own and exhibit a Pointer in the large (over 65lbs) class at the Birmingham National in 1867. The Pointer was bought in and called Ranger, age 2 years by Ranger ex Sal (Sal by Wharnby's Drake). Pointers were a specialist field sporting breed amongst the gentry, requiring particular training if they were to have any real value and James Hinks as a dog dealer, looking for quick turn around value from his stock, would not have the space or time for such field trial training commitment, although he certainly did deal in sporting field dogs that had already been broken to the gun. However, as the bull terrier breed took off in popularity, there became many breeders nationwide and no doubt some breeders may have introduced a different surreptitious backcross to try and produce their own type of new Bull Terrier.

We have seen above that Hinks upped his game in 1860 by buying in some pedigree bulldogs for line breeding and that this corresponded with the commencement of large organised dog shows. Pure white bulldogs and white "smut" bulldogs were preferred by many and were pretty common. Hinks also dealt in the White English Terrier/smooth haired terrier, some of which also carried small patches of colour. I do not particularly hold with the notion that none of these experienced breeders had an inkling that "white to white produces white". Indeed, J H Walsh wrote: *It is naturally easier to breed a pure white dog from white parents.* Establishing the white bull terrier would not, therefore, have taken long. The production of consistent type and pure white coat, as opposed to a white with patches of colour would take longer and, no doubt, the patched specimens would probably be discarded, although there is circumstantial evidence that James Hinks had a cute way of hiding these blemishes.

There was a telling report in The Field of 1st September 1866, reporting on a dog show in Halifax, which would indicate that James Hinks was not overly pleased with the coats on some of his Bull Terriers: *Bull and Terriers were represented by overly twenty as good as we should wish to see but Mr Hinks was not to be denied, as he took principal prizes though we think he would take all, if he were not to trim his dogs so much; he resorts not only to clipping but to shaving......* Clipping may indicate that a rough or broken coated terrier was in the background pedigree. As for shaving, that is a little more drastic. Could it be, perhaps, that some of them were displaying a few spots from a previous generations surreptitious dalliance with a Dalmatian, which he had to shave out of the coat!

White English Terrier

The White English Terrier was not an ancient breed but one manufactured in the 1800's to mirror the smooth coated black and tan terrier. Like Hinks's white bull terrier, the exact combination of the other breeds used is not known for certain. Hugh Dalziel, going under the pen name of "Corsincon" believed that the combination was *rather weedy fox terrier, a strong dash of bull terrier and a double dash of whippet.* Others, such as Idstone, believed that, due to the delicate nature of the White English Terrier and the fact that it lacked courage and was not up to the job of being a vermin destroyer, the Italian Greyhound was used. Bull Terrier breed books portray the White English Terrier as having become extinct with the inference being through gene degeneration. Idstone, perhaps, gives the best description saying that the White English Terrier was seldom seen, other than in the possession of dog traders and fanciers of the breed because it was bred more for show than use, *it is not a hardy nor a courageous dog.* The White English Terrier did gain in popularity for some time as a show dog but out of the ring it was always up against the attributes of the old English black and tan vermin terrier (the larger type of these developed in the North of England, later known as the Manchester Terrier, and the smaller of these developed in the South, becoming the Toy Terrier).

The breed had its ups and downs in popularity and was said to be nearly extinct then, Mr F White of Clapham Common, London propelled it back into the limelight, exhibiting no less than nine at Islington in 1862. Mr White did, however, also breed and show Bull Terriers and, no doubt, interbred with them to give his White English Terriers more substance and bottle.

The White English Terrier was also up against the new under 16lbs white bull terriers that began to appear on the show bench, which were popular in the show ring and most capable of destroying vermin. As with other breeds when large dog shows came into being, the White English Terrier underwent considerable modification. Whilst the continued crossing of the breed with Bulldogs, Bull Terriers and other smooth haired terriers meant that new genes were being introduced into the breed, in many cases, White English Terriers simply became absorbed into those other breeds. Mr Harding Cox went so far as to say that there was such a little difference between a White English and a light weight bull terrier that he was sure, in some litters, the more stocky ones were designated as bull terriers and the light weights as White English. So, in order to try and maintain the fine skulls and proper body lines, it also meant that much inbreeding was practised.

The Bull Terrier Club, subscribed to the view that the White English Terrier had become extinct, with the inference being through gene degeneration, in order that Bull Terrier owners and breeders would pay more attention to the eradication of congenital deafness which had been found to be quite widespread in the Bull Terrier. Whilst hereditary problems in trying to maintain the proper White English Terrier characteristics was most certainly a serious aspect, in reality, it would appear that the White English Terrier suffered from both becoming out of favour with terrier men, who favoured black and tan as the colour of a real vermin terrier and out of favour on the show bench. Dr Lees Bell, a great admirer of the breed put it succinctly: *While regretting extremely the decay of the White English Terrier, I am afraid they must bow to the inevitable and give place to dogs better suited to the wants and conveniences of the present day than they unfortunately are.* English White Terriers, like Bull Terriers, were cropped and the abolition of ear cropping was the final disaster – a terminal combination as it caused many of the remaining fanciers to drop the breed.

The Early Shows 1834 - 1863 (Cremorne)

As we have seen with Jemmy Shaw, the showing of dogs at sporting establishments was commonplace. When the first show of dogs at such an establishment took place we cannot say with any certainty. Certainly, the famous Charley Aistrop hosted a show of spaniels as early as 1834: *The show of nine pound spaniels for a silver cream jug will take place at Charley Aistrop's, the Elephant and Castle, Peter Street, Westminster on Wednesday, February 1834 (Toy Dogs and their ancestors, Lytton).* A Spaniel and Toy Dog Club became established at Jemmy Shaw's sporting drum at the Anchor, Bunhill Row, St Luke's, London: The Era, 28th May 1848, *Spaniel, Terrier and Small Toy Dog Fancy - a grand show or lead of these beautiful and useful little animals will take place at J Shaw's, the Blue Anchor, Bunhill Row on Thursday evening, when Mr J Ashton will preside, faced by Mr Ferriman. Fanciers are not confined to one breed alone but are earnestly invited to attend with their fancy, when every requisite can be learnt and the properties of these beautiful little creatures will be fully developed.* There are reports of such dog shows taking place in 1847, as advertised in The Era, 31st October 1847: *A show of fancy spaniels will take place at Mr Wilton's, the Prince Albert, Upper St Martin's Lane, this evening (Sunday) when some of the most celebrated dogs in London will be shown; A Terrier Show will take place at Dan Dismore's tomorrow (Monday) evening, when a silver collar will be given for competition.* The Era, 31st January 1847: *A show of small dogs (terriers) will take place at Mr Wilton's, the Prince Albert, Upper St, Martin's Lane, on Wednesday evening next.* In fact, Bells Life advertised and reported on shows of various types of dogs, including *half bred dogs* week in week out at London public houses. An annual show of Bull Terriers had been held since 1854 at the Greyhound Inn, Keymer, near Brighton.

The social aspects of Victorian life changed with the advent of the railway system, which enabled visits of previous unheard of distances to be travelled. Railway carriages provided first, second and third class accommodation, with the third class consisting of open carriages without seating. The railway network spread over the countryside, providing employment for many, including those who had previously worked on the canal system. Trunk lines were created from London to Birmingham and Liverpool and, by 1838, long distance travel by steam train was a reality between London, Birmingham, Manchester and Preston. By the 1860's and 1870's, the railway network had also become a means by which dog stealers and dog dealers could move dogs with ease around the country, from town to town and abroad, as James Hinks is known to have done.

Dog stealing became a rife and very lucrative way for the low life to earn money. They would simply steal a dog and either return it for the reward offered or sell the dog on to a dog dealer. In some cases they would simply contact the owner saying that they would return the dog for a sum of money, otherwise it would be poisoned. This activity reached such proportions that an Act of Parliament, The Dog Stealing Act (also popularly known as the Bishop's Act) was passed in 1845, the Act was later amended to strengthen the penalties that magistrates could impose and The Society for the Prosecution of Dog Stealers and their Confederates was formed to support in the prosecution of offenders. The extension of the railway network created another aspect to dog stealing, whereby a dog could be stolen in Manchester in the morning and be sold in Birmingham or London later that day with little hope of the owner finding it. In fact, at a Court case in Ashton, near Manchester, in early 1870, James Hinks was allegedly named as one of the central figures in an international dog stealing fraternity. This case will be reviewed in detail when considering the possible reasons for his withdrawal from the dog show scene.

It was only a matter of time before the inventive Victorians were to introduce large scale dog shows organised on an entrepreneurial basis. The first two of such shows were held in 1859, at Newcastle and the other in Birmingham. However, these shows were confined to sporting (field) dogs.

As previously discussed, The National Exhibition of sporting and other dogs was held at Midland Counties Repository in Birmingham in December 1860. Only one prize per breed was offered. The winning dogs at the show were not named, only the name of the owner/exhibitor was given. There was a class for Bulldogs with five entries, James Hinks winning the Bulldog class. Contemporary evidence clearly proving that Hinks's winning bulldog was a bitch, correcting an error in the breed's history that has endured for some 160 years.

On Easter Monday, 1st April 1861, a small Exhibition of Fancy Dogs took place in a wooden pavilion at the rear of the Nags Head, Lichfield Street, Birmingham. In large size Bulldogs, James Hinks won both first and second prizes (winning animals unfortunately not named). He also took first prizes in the classes for large Bull Terriers and Toy Bull Terriers (winning animals not named). The event was so successful that the Landlord of the Inn and organiser of the show, Mr Sprawson, quickly followed up with another Exhibition of Fancy Dogs in August 1861.

In July 1861, The North of England Exhibition of sporting and other dogs was held as an add on to the Royal Agricultural Society show in Leeds. There were classes for Bulldogs, 1st Mr H Fearn's Rush [2711] who beat her sire, Mr T Spencer's Spring [2649] into second place. Taking third place was Mr H Brown's dog, Crib, from London. Mr Brown, Landlord of the Sugar Loaf Inn, King Street, Drury Lane, was one of the London school of "old doggy men" and not being satisfied at his defeat by a bulldog from the country, issued a challenge to Mr Fearn in Bells Life: *CHALLENGE TO ALL ENGLAND – J Ferriman is authorised to show the bulldog Crib, belonging to H Brown, against any other dog or bitch living for from £5 to £100, Mr Fearn's bitch of Sheffield preferred.* As previously noted, James Hinks was later to buy this bulldog bitch, Rush [2711] from Mr Fearn. In Bull Terriers, Mr Hustwick took both 1st and 2nd places with Violet and Jess. There were no KC Stud Book entries for bull terriers at this show.

The second Nag's Head show, Lichfield Street, Birmingham took place at the end of August 1861. At this show James Hinks entered and was successful in several breeds, as reported in Bells Life: *Mr Hinks of 4 Phillip Street, Market Hall, Birmingham was the most successful, carrying off the first prize of a silver cup for a splendid specimen of the bull bitch* (presumably his bulldog bitch Madman) *and second prize for Bulldog; also a first prize for bull terrier bitch and second prize for bull terrier dog.*

The first Holborn dog show was held in the first week of October 1861. However, the prize money offered for non sporting dogs was so much out of proportion to those offered for sporting dogs that the London school of "old doggy men" decided to organise their own show in direct competition with the toffs show. So it was that the first Holborn Show clashed with The North London Dog Show, organised by Mr Ferriman and his cohorts at his Graham Arms, in City Road, the saloon of which was capable of containing 400 dogs. The Era reported that Mr Ferriman's show *chiefly represented the London Fancy, some of the leading names being connected with it. Consequently, a number of very choice animals indeed were divided between the two places.*

Both these shows provided separate classes for bull terriers. James Hinks exhibited at the North London Dog Show, perhaps being encouraged to attend by Mr Ferriman from whom he had bought a bulldog bitch in 1858. This was probably the first show at which both James Hinks and Bill Tupper exhibited against each other in bulldogs – Bill Tupper easily won the day with all the main winners coming down from Tupper's stud dog, Frank [2622], who was also amongst the prize winners. James Hinks did win first prize and a silver collar with his bull terrier, a white dog called Turk, second in the class was a white bitch, owned by Mr Mills called Beauty. Mr Ferriman won both first and second prizes in bull terriers under 7lbs with his ratting dogs, Gas and Dick.

At the Holborn Show the large size bulldog class was won by Percival's Captain (by Percival's Toss ex Duchess and therefore a half brother of Carey's Charlie, who was the sire of Holland's Poll). Mr William McDonald was clearly not one of the London school of "old doggy men" as he chose to attend and exhibit at the Holborn Show and won a first prize with his under 10lbs Bulldog called Tiny. Mr McDonald is reviewed because, in the alternative "there was no fight" theory, Mr McDonald, we are told, was a London friend of James Hinks. This may well have been so, they exhibited many times at the same shows with various breeds, including bulldogs and bull terriers. The bull terrier winner at Holborn was Mr Godson's white bitch, Queen.

The Second Exhibition of sporting and other dogs at Birmingham was held in December 1861. There were, again, no classes for Bull Terriers but there was a class for Bulldogs. Taking 1st was Mr Lamphier's King Dick [2633] 2nd was James Hinks's bitch Madman [2690] and in 3rd place Mr Percival's Captain.

Hinks was also awarded a highly commended with Rose. At the same show Mr W McDonald's white Bulldog Tiny was awarded an extra prize and was also in the cards with a King Charles Spaniel.

Manchester held a First Exhibition of sporting and other dogs in December 1861 at the Belle Vue Zoological Gardens. There were classes for Bulldogs and Bull Terriers. Unfortunately, the winning dogs were not named with only the names of the owners/exhibitors being given. There were four placings for Bull Terriers, taken respectively by Messrs Howarth, Gregson, Burmiston and Shepherd.

The Holborn Show 1862

The second Holborn Horse Repository and dog show in 1862 has caused much controversy and confusion for bull terrier enthusiasts and breed historians, many of whom have tied themselves in knots, so it is best to clear up a couple of these points with definitively correct and verifiable historic answers. Firstly, for whatever reason, this show was not included by the Kennel Club when compiling details of shows held between 1859 and 1873, so there are no Stud Book entries, which is a great shame. Some writers quote extensively from other breed history books variously: that Cremorne,1863 *was the first London Show to offer classes for the breed* (Montgomery, The Bull Terrier); Montgomery no doubt getting this gem from Haynes: *Not only was this the first London Show to recognise the breed by giving it a separate classification, but it was also the first show at which Hinks family appear as exhibitors* (William Haynes, The Bull Terrier, 1912). This also gave rise to the various statements that Puss was first shown at Cremorne in 1863; that *there are no records which have either Cremorne or Holborn as the location of a dog show in 1862* (Lane, Dog Shows and Doggy People, 1902); that Farman reinforced Lane's claim of there *being only two shows in 1862, one at Islington and one at Birmingham* (Farman, The Bulldog, 1903); and that *I have to reject the existence of a dog show at Holborn in 1862* (Kane, Pity Me, 1999). This is a clear example of writers conforming to what has gone before. As we have seen above, the first Holborn show and The North London Dog Show in October 1861 were equal first in recognising bull terriers by giving the breed a separate classification and The North London Dog Show was the first London show at which the Hinks family appeared as exhibitors.

Some modern writers have tied themselves in knots by promoting an alternative theory that "there was no fight" (at Tupper's in Long Acre) and writing that the dog show at Holborn in 1862 did not even take place. What does this suggest about the respected Rawden Lee – that his account, written in 1889, was a complete and utter fabrication from start to finish! These scenarios are reviewed in detail later and the balance of probability arrived at using contemporary sources from the 1860's. In the meantime here are the facts on the existence of the second Holborn Show:

The first day of the second Holborn Horse Repository and dog show (The Holborn Show) was Monday, 26th May 1862. The organisers of the Holborn show were keen to promote its dog section and learning from the previous year's show, breeders and owners of non sporting breeds were attracted to enter the show by the very high prize money on offer, particularly for bulldogs and bull terriers. Holborn 1862 was the first show where Puss was named in the prize list as having been exhibited. There were full reports of the Holborn Show in London newspapers, such as London Reynolds, Penny Newsman, Bells Life, The Era and Illustrated London News. The Era in its issue on Sunday 1st June 1862 reported:

> *Rarely has such a treat been offered to the admirers of the canine race as that on view at the Holborn Horse Repository during the past week and the amount of public patronage bestowed.....The Managers offered prizes to no fewer than thirty four classes of dogs and the heaviest sums were offered for large size Bulldogs and Bull Terriers and these were awarded respectively to Mr Hinks Madman and Mr Hinks Puss, the former being the truest type of the Bull species that we have seen for some time........*
>
> *Bulldogs (large size)- 1st prize, £10, Mr Hinks's Madman; 2nd prize, £4, Mr Tupper's Nell; 3rd prize, £2, Mr Hinks's Nelson;*
>
> *Bulldogs (small) – 1st prize, £10, Mr McDonald's Lady; 2nd prize, £4, Mr McDonald's Tiny; 3rd prize, £2, Mr Nash's Little Wonder;*
>
> *Bull Terriers – 1st prize, £10, Mr Hinks's Puss; 2nd prize £4, Mr Edmond's Don; 3rd prize, £2, Mr McDonald's Nettle.*

Hinks's bulldog bitch Madman beat Bill Tupper's bulldog bitch, Nell, into second place. It is said that there was an apparent argument between the gentlemen. Certainly Bill Tupper, as we later see from his character traits, would not have been happy being beaten by a person from the country and he would have had support from the other London school of "old doggy men". Mr McDonald was apparently not a member of the London school of "old doggy men" and it was after the Holborn Show that Mr W McDonald invited James Hinks to be the Chairman at a show of Toy dogs at his Caledonian and Scotch Stores in Long Acre, London on 1st June 1862. This is also discussed further when reviewing the Puss fight in detail.

The London school of "old doggy men" consolidated their support behind Bill Tupper because, in June 1862, two shows followed in London within a week and James Hinks exhibited at both. The first being what was now billed as "Ferriman's Dog Show", again held at the Graham Arms in City Road on 18th June 1862. Mr H Brown won the Bulldog class with his Crib, the large size Bull Terrier class with Janey and also the small bull terrier class with Gas. Mr Ferriman, himself, being second with his bull terrier, Dick. James Hinks did not win any prizes in either bulldogs or bull terriers. All he managed was a second prize with a red rough terrier.

The second show in June 1862 was The North of England Second Exhibition of sporting and other dogs held over four days from 24th to 28th June, at the New Agricultural Hall in Islington, London. Unfortunately for James Hinks, the bulldog and bull terrier judge was none other than Mr H Brown, one of Ferriman's friends from the London school of "old doggy men" who apparently and quite arrogantly brought his own dog Crib into the ring to show the crowd what a good bulldog should really look like. James Hinks was placed third with his bulldog bitch Madman [2690], 1st was Mr J Lamphier's King Dick [2633] and 2nd was Bill George with his Dan [2610]. Whilst this judging may have been correct, because Hinks's bulldog bitch Madman had previously stood behind Lamphier's King Dick, in bull terriers the Judge also did not favour Hinks who received only a highly commended for his bull terrier (presumably this was Puss who had won at Holborn the previous month). The three placings for bull terriers were taken respectively by Mr Cross with Duchess, Mr Edmon's with Don and Mr F White (the well known English White Terrier man) with Rattler, all of whom were London based exhibitors. The breeder of Mr White's Rattler (born in 1861 by Rattler ex Duchess) was Bill Tupper.

So ended Hinks' dalliance with the London school of "old doggy men". It was clear that he was on a hiding to nothing by continuing to exhibit at shows organised by Ferriman and the London school of "old doggy men" who just used the upstart from the country as exhibition fodder.

The Islington show became infamous and for a while cast a shadow over subsequent large events because the winners were swindled out of their prize money by the organiser, Mr Appleby. He hailed from Leeds and, found to be a failed cheesemonger, was thereafter referred to as "the Yorkshire cheesemonger". The show was said to be a fraud or a hoax. It was billed as The North of England Second Exhibition of sporting and other dogs but it should have been called "the Appleby show" as it was financed and organised by Mr Appleby, who appointed himself secretary and formed a committee of one, duping the good and great to be Patrons of the show for a fee. Mr Appleby's apparent aim was that the Islington Show would make a great profit and cover his other business debts. So, how did he get away with it ?

Mr Appleby was able to achieve his aims because he had built a good reputation, having been responsible for the entire management of the successful Leeds Dog Show in 1861 and also the Leeds Horticultural and Floral Exhibition. The Islington Show was a success with over 1,000 dogs being entered and very popular amongst the viewing public with around £3,000 taken on the door and through entries. Many dogs were sold at the show, with Mr Appleby receiving the funds of £800 to £900, which he was to pass over to the vendors after taking his ten percent fee. Although awards were made on the day and everything appeared to go smoothly, when the day came for actually paying out the prize money and giving out the cups, Mr Appleby had vanished. The prizes had been sent back to the makers and both prize money and the money made from selling dogs was withheld. Instead of their prize, the winners received a letter: *I regret having to inform you that, owing to the heavy losses Mr Thomas Dawkins Appleby, of this town, cheese and bacon factor, has sustained, he is compelled to suspend payment. I am, therefore, directed to call a meeting of his creditors, to be held at the Griffin Hotel, Leeds, on Friday next, the 11th instant, at twelve o'clock at noon, when Mr Appleby will submit a statement of his affairs to the meeting and be prepared to take such steps as shall be considered advisable for the benefit of his creditors.*

Mr McDonald travelled from London to attend and voice his views at the creditors meeting in Leeds and, on his return, held a meeting of the affected London exhibitors at his Caledonian Hall, in Long Acre, to advise of events and to see what steps could be taken *for the protection of gentlemen who patronise the canine race.* It was proposed that future shows had to guarantee that prize money and prizes would be paid and Patrons were to pay more than lip service for the receipt of their fee. Mr McDonald's actions following the Islington show in 1862 promoted him to such an extent that he would be appointed Manager of the non sporting section at the next Islington show. Mr McDonald appeared well suited to self promotion to the extent of having copper coins of a monetary value struck at his own expense for use over the bar and no doubt for betting at sporting events at his Caledonian Hall and Scotch Stores.

The Islington show was also the start of the death knell for ear cropping. Sir Edwin Landseer was one of the judges at the show and his suggestion, that *in future no dogs with cropped ears, or otherwise mutilated, shall be admitted into shows* was taken up by the leading paper of the day, The Times: *We trust that the suggestion of Sir Edwin Landseer will be adopted.......the cropping system is a piece of unnecessary cruelty and bad taste........if dog shows should lead to the abandonment of this common but absurd and cruel practice, they will have produced an unforeseen and very gratifying result.* Thus the bandwagon against ear cropping commenced but would take some thirty years before its aims were fully achieved.

The first four days in December 1862 saw the Third Exhibition of sporting and other dogs held at the Old Wharf in Birmingham. Still no class for Bull Terriers at Birmingham but the Bulldog class was again won by Mr Lamphier's King Dick. James Hinks took both 2nd and 3rd places with Nelson [2637] born in 1862 (by Lamphier's King Dick ex Holland's Poll) and Rose [2709] born in 1860 (by Carey's Charlie ex Carey's Nettle). Mr McDonald again picking up an extra prize for his Tiny. In Dalmatian's, James Hinks name appears for the first time, winning an extra prize with his home bred Spot [2577] born in 1862 (by Joss ex Dinah). Mr W McDonald was in the cards again, this time with a Dandie Dinmont called Duchess, Scotch Terriers, Flora and Jannett, King Charles Spaniels, Pet and Lola Montes and his Blenheim Spaniel.

The First Annual Grand National Exhibition of sporting and other dogs was held in Ashburnham Hall, Cremorne, Chelsea 23rd to 28th March 1863 (The Cremorne Show). It is during the course of the Cremorne show that, on the balance of probability, the Puss fight took place. In large size Bull Terriers, sixty dogs were exhibited, with James Hinks being 1st with Puss [2821] (by Rebel ex Wasp), 2nd was Mr West's Nell [2816], 3rd Mr Jackson's Tip.

Large size Bulldogs saw an entry of 39, with Mr Lamphier's King Dick taking 1st, 2nd was Mr McDonald with Wasp [2718] and 3rd Mr Pike with Lord Nelson [2637] (James Hinks having sold Nelson to Mr Pike who changed its name to Lord Nelson). In the under 18lbs class, Bill Tupper took 1st with Floss [2678] and 3rd with Frank [2622], 2nd place was Mr F White's Crook [2608] (sired by Tupper's stud dog, Frank [2622]). Mr McDonald was in the cards again with a White Scotch Terrier, Flo and James Hinks was also in the cards with a Fawn Scotch Terrier, Gipsy.

Puss, that fight and the future

When Puss appeared at dog shows in 1862 and 1863, the objection by the owners of the bulldog and old style bull-terrier to Hinks' new dog could not have been to her colour. White Bulldogs were common and preferred by many and a white bull and terrier was also common. Captain Browne in his book Anecdotes of Dogs, published in 1829, appears to be the first to have penned a description of a dog under the name of bull terrier and notes that they were often white: *He has rather a large, square head, short neck, deep chest and very strong legs. He possesses great strength of jaw and draws a badger with much ease. He is of all colours but often white, with large black or brown patches on different parts of his body. His hair is short and stiff.* R H Glyn refers to the Freeborn family of Oxford having a kennel of white bull and terriers in the 1830's. A review of dog show reports in Bells Life reveals many white bull terriers including that in April 1860: *A show of dogs will take place this evening, April 15, at F Banham's the Bricklayers Arms, King's Road, Chelsea, Mr E Smart will take the chair and will produce his stud of white Bull Terriers.* Mr Smart was landlord of the Peacock Inn, Vauxhall Walk, London.

When Puss appeared, the objection, possibly, may have been to her "type". I have not read of many first hand descriptions of very early bull terriers in breed history books. However, we can thank Bells Life for their reports of an 1864 dog show at Alexandra Park, where the Madman litter brothers, Turk, Puss and Daisy were exhibited: *These are all white terriers of the same character, neat, short dogs, with a peculiar long head which, with the close cropped ears, gave them rather a vulgar than a handsome look.* A report at Birmingham the same year gave an idea of the expression: *White with fine skins, good heads and sharp eyes.* So, Puss was clean limbed, neat and short in body, probably a little lighter in build than the regular bull-terrier and certainly a longer refined head compared to her counterparts, though still lippy.

However, I do not believe that either of these two theories is correct. I simply believe that Bill Tupper, supported by the other London school of "old doggy men" decided to teach the upstart from the country a lesson putting both Hinks's reputation and that of his new type of bull terrier on the line. As we will see, Bill Tupper's character was such that he would want revenge for his defeat to Hinks's bulldog bitch at Holborn. Hinks had always previously been beaten by Tupper's bulldogs or dogs sired by Tupper's stud dog. So whilst comments of admiration were made about Puss, it was also said that, perhaps, this white dog was now too soft to make the scratch. Here is where the intrigue, confusion and controversy starts, WAS THERE A FIGHT OR NOT?

We must start with the nearest thing to a record, Mr Rawdon B Lee's account of the fight. Mr Lee was the Editor of "The Field" and also a respected author but more than that, Mr Lee was a bull terrier man, having won a first prize with his "Madman" [2739] (by Walker's Crib ex Roocroft's Puss, Crib being sired by Hinks' famous Madman [2740]) at The First Scottish Metropolitan Exhibition of sporting and fancy dogs held in Edinburgh, 1871, in the over 18lbs class, gaining his "Madman" a KC stud book entry.

> *It was early in the (eighteen) fifties that James Hinks began to cross the patched, heavy headed bull terrier, used for fighting, with the English White Terrier and in time he produced dogs handsome enough to make a name for themselves and be able to revolutionise the variety. Some of the old "doggy men" said that this new breed were soft and could not fight. "can't they?" said Hinks, when talking to a lot of his London friends at the Holborn Horse Repository dog show in May 1862. "I think they can." "Well," said one of the London school, "Let's make a match." Hinks, nothing more loth, did make a match and backed his bitch Puss – that day she had won first prize in her class – for £5 and a case of champagne, against one of the short faced patched dogs similar in weight. The fight came off the same evening at Bill Tupper's well-known rendezvous in Long Acre. It took Puss half an hour to kill her opponent and so little the worse was she for her encounter that she appeared on the bench next morning, a few marks on her cheeks and muzzle being the only signs of the determined combat in which she had been the principal over night. When accounts of this became bruited abroad, although it was not generally believed, the popularity of the "long faced" dog was established.*

I found this a somewhat intriguing conundrum and decided to research the balance of probability using contemporary sources from the 1860's. The alternative theory says that Rawden B Lee's account of the event had factual inaccuracies and that historians of the breed were in effect lazy because they relied on anecdotal evidence. This is somewhat disingenuous to our respected breed historians because the account of the incident could not be reported on at the time and it would only ever be able to be discussed in closed circle of those "in the know" because dog fighting was illegal.

I have found the alternative theory to be fatally flawed. The alternative theory tells us that anecdotal evidence is the weakest form of evidence since it relies on word of mouth. This calls in to question the basis of the alternative theory itself. Was this not also purely based on anecdotal evidence – that the fight was said to have taken place during the period of the Holborn Horse Repository and dog show in 1862 (the "Holborn Show"). Mr R H Glyn, one of the most respected breed historians, clearly states in his book "Bull Terriers and how to breed them" first published in May 1936, that the fight DID NOT take place at the Holborn Show in 1862, as written by Mr Lee, but the following year at the large "Cremorne Show" (The First Annual Grand National Exhibition of sporting and other dogs) held in the Ashburnham Hall, Cremorne, Chelsea, 23rd to 28th March 1863): *I know of no other authority who does not either agree that a fight took place after the Cremorne show, or else borrows flagrantly from Lee.* The alternative "there was no fight" theory does borrow flagrantly from Lee.

William ("Bill") Tupper

In considering the balance of probability that the Puss fight did take place, we need to look at the other main protagonist, Bill Tupper. Now Bill Tupper was no mug, nor was he ever a bit part player. He was most certainly, along with James Ferriman and Harry Brown, one of the London school of "old doggy men". In fact, Bill Tupper was a well known London "sporting" raconteur with a growing reputation. He was involved in all things sporting from boxing to bulldogs and from rats to pigeons. He was an extremely well known London dealer of several breeds including "sporting dogs". He had a particular interest in bulldogs and in 1856 acquired a small bulldog of only 12lbs called Nottingham Frank. Bill Tupper sent many under 18lbs bulldogs to France where they were much admired. These small bulldogs would have given partly to the development of the French Bulldog and Bill Tupper is mentioned in French Bulldog history books.

Let us be under no illusion, the new large dog shows were a great market place for advertising and selling puppies, dogs and dogs for stud. There would be and was great rivalry between owners, breeders and, particularly dog dealers, that extended beyond these shores and the rewards if a person was dealing in several breeds, as James Hinks, Bill Tupper and William McDonald were, would be potentially great. There would have been a natural friendly rivalry between some exhibitors and a more vitriolic rivalry amongst others. Some rivalry would, no doubt, occasionally spoil over into bad blood which would be settled in some way acceptable to the parties, either in public or private, legal or illegal. Bull Terriers were not the only breed to be developed for show purposes, bulldogs had also changed. This was reported on in Bells Life coverage of the Cremorne Show in 1863: *Several of the specimens in the two last classes were very fine but we endorse an opinion that has been expressed by many good judges that the old breed of English Bulldogs is sadly degenerated....*

Unlike Mr McDonald, Bill Tupper did not appear to exhibit at the early dog shows outside London. Mr Tupper did, however, make trips out of London to rat killing contests, including to Birmingham and Nottingham. It appears that Tupper and Hinks exhibited against each other with Bulldogs for the first time at The North London Dog Show in October 1861. Bill Tupper easily won the day in bulldogs with all the main winners coming down from Tupper's stud dog, Frank [2622].

When large organised showcase dog shows came into being Bill Tupper would again expect to clean up on prizes at the London shows, enhance his reputation and his sales then, James Hinks, the interloper from the country, appears at the Holborn Show in May 1862, with probably the same bulldogs that Tupper had vanquished six months earlier but the judge in the bulldogs (large size) class favoured James Hinks' bulldog bitch Madman over Bill Tupper's bitch Nell who was placed second. In the bulldogs (small) class, Bill Tupper was also pushed out by his London rival, William McDonald, who took the first prize with Lady and the second prize with Tiny. Bill Tupper believed that Hinks' bulldog was inferior to his own. Not only that but James Hinks walked off with £22 in prize money, whilst Tupper pocketed only £4.

Bill Tupper was apparently not well pleased and it is alleged that an argument ensued between Bill Tupper and James Hinks in relation to bulldogs. This would not be an uncommon occurrence because there was generally much dispute and discussion as to what a "good" bulldog should look like and there were generally three sizes of bulldog, many being half or three quarter bred. It would appear that the bad blood between James Hinks and Bill Tupper therefore probably may have started at the Holborn Show in May 1862 but the bad blood actually came to a head at the Cremorne show in March 1863.

Mr McDonald was not only a rival London bulldog breeder and a rival dog dealer, he was also a local business rival of Bill Tupper's. It may be that Mr McDonald saw an opportunity to "rub Tupper's nose in it" by inviting James Hinks to be the Chairman at a show of Toy dogs at his Caledonian and Scotch Stores in Long Acre, London on 1st June 1862. Take this advert in 1st June 1862 issue of Bells Life as rubbing salt into Bill Tupper's wound: *The Caledonian Hall Scotch Stores 27 Long Acre will be opened this evening.... Mr Hinks of Birmingham in the chair, who will show his two bulldogs and bull terrier that obtained the first prizes at the Holborn Exhibition....... W McDonald will also show his two toy bulldogs which took first and second prizes and will be prepared to show them against anything in England for the properties of a bulldog of their weight....W McDonald especially invites gentlemen to attend this show, being one of the best of the year, including most of the best dogs in London of their respective classes.* This rubbing of Tupper's nose in it proved to be a great mistake for Mr McDonald, as we shall see later.

That same evening, Bill Tupper was vice chair at a show of dogs to be held at the Queen's Head, London Road, Southwark, which was also advertised in Bells Life: *Chair taken by H Jones, vice Mr Tupper who will show his bull bitch Nell, that took the prize at the Holborn Show.* Note "the prize", Bill Tupper and his associates obviously dismissing his second place to Hinks's bulldog.

Bill Tupper was also involved in Boxing, his "sporting drum" being used where the boxers and their promoters would meet and pay over the stake money and side bets to the stakeholder. The stakeholder was often Bells Life. One of these boxing events was the championship match between Goss and Mace for a purse of £2,000 Bill Tupper was actively supporting Goss, who used his establishment as a base prior to the boxing match and also trained at Bill Tupper's family country property in Ash, near Aldershot.

In another example of his character trait, reported on in Bells Life, 17th May 1863: *Tupper and Wilson – the match between Mr Tupper's dog Pincher and Mr Wilson's dog Rock to destroy 100 rats each, for £25 a side, took place at Nottingham last week. Pincher's time was 10min 6sec and Rock's 9min 3sec..... Mr Tupper, not being satisfied with his defeat, nor treatment at Nottingham, will again back his dog Pincher against the Nottingham dog Rock, to destroy 100 or 200 rats for £25 or £50 a side and give £3 for the match to come off in London. Bells Life to be the stakeholder.* Bells Life 17th October 1863: *In answer to Mr Heath's enquiry last week, as to which is the champion ratter, Mr W Tupper wishes to state that he considers his Pincher the holder of that title, to prove which he will match Pincher against any dog in the world at 100 rats, for £25 a side; or he will destroy 110 against Mr Heath's Kit's 100, for a like sum.* Mr Heath was the landlord of the Hop Pole, Lawley Street, which was a sporting drum in Birmingham.

Bill Tupper was a man who hated to lose and acted adversely in defeat. He could not stand being beaten by what he deemed Hinks's inferior bulldog at the Holborn show in 1862 and that he won only £4 in prize money, whereas Hinks pocketed £22, so sought to teach the upstart from the country a lesson.

The Puss Fight at Tupper's Blue Boars Head, Long Acre

To be absolutely clear and strictly pragmatic and fair, I will apply the same stringent tests to the Cremorne Show in 1863, that the alternative theory applied to the Holborn Show in 1862 and see where that takes us. Readers can then decide for themselves whether they believe that, on the balance of probability, the account by Rawdon B Lee, save for the date, is correct and the fight did, in fact, take place at Bill Tupper's Blue Boars Head, in Long Acre, as he generally described.

Firstly, were the main protagonists in attendance at the Cremorne Show?

The Report for the Cremorne Show, in March 1863 and the prize list for the show discloses that Bill Tupper had two bulldogs in the cards that day, both in the under 18lbs class. The first was a bitch called Floss who won a first prize. Bill Tupper later sold this bitch to Mr F Else who continued to show her. The other was Bill Tupper's "famous" stud dog called Frank who won a third prize. In bull terriers, James Hinks is shown as having won a first prize, valued at £5, with Puss. The other gentleman on whom the alternative theory places importance was also present at the Cremorne Show. This was Mr W McDonald, who won a second prize with his bulldog bitch, Wasp, in the large class. So, all the protagonists were present at the Cremorne Show in 1863 with Puss indeed winning (as written by Rawden B Lee) a first prize to the value of £5. The first test is passed.

Secondly, did the fight take place at Bill Tupper's "well known rendezvous in Long Acre"?

The alternative theory and those that choose to promote the belief that there was no fight lay great store in the "facts" that Bill Tupper did not own a public house in Long Acre and that Long Acre would, in any case, not have been a suitable area for such a venue because it was too prestigious a location. The indisputable verifiable fact is that Bill Tupper actually became the owner of the Blue Boar's Head, Long Acre, in early February 1863, more than a month before the Cremorne Show. As to Bill Tupper's Blue Boar Head being "a well known rendezvous" – so it was. Bill Tupper's Blue Boar's Head (also called the Blue Boar or the Pig's Head) in Long Acre received many mentions in Bells Life for being the *sporting drum for knows* (and read into that what you will).

For a six month period in 1863, until he sold the Greyhound Inn, Bill Tupper owned both the Greyhound in Webber Row and the Blue Boar in Long Acre. We know this as a sure fact because in the 15th February 1863 issue of Bells Life the following was reported: *A show of dogs takes place this evening, Feb 15, at W Tupper's the Greyhound, Webber Row, Waterloo Road........ Mr T has taken the Blue Boar's Head, Long Acre. Due notice will be given of the opening.*

As for Long Acre being too prestigious an area for such a venue, as we will see, Bill Tupper's Blue Boar's Head was not the only "sporting drum" in Long Acre. So, at the time of the Cremorne show, Bill Tupper (as written by Rawden B Lee) did own the Blue Boar's Head in Long Acre and the Inn was conveniently, for the purposes of an illegal dog fight, not open to the public – the second test is passed.

Thirdly, the alternative theory tells us that, at dog shows, the owner of the dog had to deposit the dog at the show and then leave (in practise, many exhibits were sent by carriage or train and the "Keepers" collected them and took them to the show). The Keepers then fed, watered, exercised and exhibited the dogs and the owner could not remove the dog until judging and the viewing by the public were completed and this could take several days. So, was this the case?

The manager of Cremorne Gardens and the proprietor of the Cremorne show was Mr E T Smith. Mr Smith had many ventures prior to becoming manager at Cremorne: he had been a Bow Street Runner; a Sherriff's Bailiff; an auctioneer; tried his hand in the wine trade; and then as landlord of the Red Lion in Holborn (where he dressed the barmaids in bloomers); he became a theatre manager and a restaurant owner. Some of the ventures were successful and others were dismal failures. Mr Smith was said to have *little money of his own........but with friends who believed in his speculative flair.* He was also said to be *an interesting man, of boundless energy and resource and a lucky, if wayward, speculator, who was everything by turns and nothing long.* In other words, Mr Smith was a bit of a chancer.

Bill Tupper was an associate of E T Smith. Again, as reported in the 15th February issue of Bells Life: *The full tip of the great dog show at Ashburnham Hall (Cremorne) can be had at Mr Tupper's, as he is authorised so to do by Mr E T Smith.* So, Bill Tupper would, perhaps, have had influence amongst the show's organisers and staff. It is reasonable to surmise that the local London Keepers' would probably personally know Bill Tupper, or certainly know of him, they would be paid a pittance for their duties as Keepers' and a couple of them may well have helped to spirit Puss out of Ashburnham Hall and back in again for either a "good turn" or more likely, a paid inducement. The show did not open to the public until 12 noon each day, providing ample time for Puss to have been washed down after her fight the previous evening and transported back to Ashburnham Hall for the following afternoon's viewing by spectators.

Newspaper reports in Bells Life, London Reynolds and the Penny Newsman all make it clear that the organisation of these early dog shows left much to be desired, with the Penny Newsman reporting of one such show: *It was announced in Bells Life that most of the prize dogs would be exhibited at the various sporting houses so, "with leave or without leave" they would have them away.* There appeared, therefore, to be somewhat of a disregard for the show organisers regulations that exhibits remain in the precincts of the show until allowed out. It is also reported that at the early shows, some dogs escaped from their cages and went missing. Circumstances favoured the third test being satisfied in that: at the early shows dogs did go "missing"; Bill Tupper would certainly not be without influence with the local London Keepers'; and there was adequate time for both Puss to be secreted out of the show the previous evening and back in again prior to 12 noon the following day.

Fourthly, what of the marks on Puss the following day, which the alternative theory suggests would have caused some consternation and complaint amongst middle class spectators?

This is a somewhat particularly silly point. You cannot apply 20th/21st century politically correct sentimentality to 19th century incidents. In the 1860's bull terriers and several other breeds were traditionally cropped and I would have thought that, at that time, marks on many of the dog breeds and particularly bull breeds would certainly not be out of the ordinary. We should also remember that this was the new age of Exhibitions and organised dog shows and many middle class spectators would have gone along to "gape" pretty much in awe, the same way as visiting a Zoo for the first time. Take these examples of the type of dog they experienced for the first time, as reported in Bells Life *The foreign hounds were simple curiosities that, so far as this country is concerned, might just as well be kept in glass cases; the ferocity of an Australian bred animal but of a breed that is unknown, at least to us, kept his audience at a distance.*

Spectators may be seeing some breeds of dog close up for the first time, knowing them only by reputation. Others may well have previously visited "sporting drum's" in Long Acre and elsewhere in London and would not view a few marks on a bull terrier type of dog as being either unexpected or untoward. The report of the Cremorne show in the London Morning Post discloses that, for exercise, *ten brace at a time were led out to stretch their legs and allay the excitement created by their being chained up so long in a place where their passions were every minute being aroused by their neighbouring friends.* This certainly looks like a recipe for close contact by excitable dogs and provides the opportunity for certain minded exhibits of any breed to put a couple of marks on each other. Furthermore, the comment on the bulldogs in the London Morning Post: *The bulldogs, from their ugliness, would have satisfied any Whitechapel coalheaver or shiffnall collier and the record of their battles were hung up over them...* Also, Mr Percival, the bull terrier judge at Cremorne, had his famous bull terrier Captain benched, with the Sporting Life reporter commenting: *He is one of the most perfect of the half bred dogs ever seen – he is brindled pied. The list of battles that he has won figure on a conspicuous card over his head – he is in his fifth year.* So, with these facts in mind, I certainly do not believe that a few marks on a bull terrier would be considered out of the ordinary and in 1863 would, in any case, lead more to aghast admiration rather than complaint. The fourth test is passed.

What then of the fifth and final test that Mr W McDonald would not have invited James Hinks to take the Chair as a judge at a dog show held at the

Caledonian Scotch Stores, 27 Long Acre, London in June 1862 if he believed that James Hinks was involved in dog fighting. In the alternative theory, Mr McDonald, we are told, was a London friend of James Hinks, was himself a reputable show manager and proprietor of the Caledonian Scotch Stores in Long Acre and was portrayed in the alternative theory as a highly respected gentleman among the London middle classes and could not risk his reputation being tarnished by association.

The fifth and final stringent test is very easily satisfied. It took very little research time to reveal that Mr W McDonald's Caledonian Hall at 27 Long Acre, London was also a well known "sporting drum". Mr McDonald may have mixed with the "highs" but was also very adept at mixing with the "lows". Take these extracts from Bells Life as evidence: *On Wednesday evening the match for W McDonald's bitch to destroy 50 rats in five minutes will take place. Gentlemen are respectfully solicited to be early for the time nine o'clock will be strictly kept.......gentlemen wishing to "try" their dogs on these nights can do so, a plentiful supply of rats being provided." "W McD's bitch Nell will on Wednesday August 26 destroy 100 rats against time, viz eight minutes and on Wednesday Sept 9, her match to destroy 50 rats against the Cheltenham bitch Patch, at the above house, will take place..........*

So much for Long Acre being too prestigious a location for such venues. Further clear evidence of regular dog fights in Long Acre comes from the 17th September 1864 issue of Penny Illustrated Paper, commenting on an article about a dog "show" on a Sunday evening, from the Daily News: *First to the back parlour of a tavern in Long Acre, when just as the adjacent church, St Paul's, Covent Garden, is discharging its congregation and when a fair proportion of the pedestrians you meet have prayer books in their hands, the so called "show" is going on. There is neither let nor hinderance to your admission. You are asked to walk in by a gentleman at the bar and you soon find yourself one of a mixed company of a dozen or so. Five of these are men, the rest dogs. The rattling of chairs proceeds from the dogs, the oaths and strong language from the men. The former are chained to iron rings fixed in the wall or to the legs of the table at which the latter sit, or else share the table with tumblers of gin and watery pewter tankards of beer and clay pipes and tobacco. The "show" is very like a tap room and the guests are a rough and ready plain spoken set. They call spades spades very frequently during your stay, tell you of the bobbies having stopped a fight which was to "ave come off near the Welsh Arp this very Sunday morning." Reminiscences of other fights not stopped, whereas speakers looked on, anticipations of a great ratting match to come, speculations as to the victor and hope for the guv'nor's success follow this and then you hear under the moist seal of tavern confidence of a coming dog fight, which you will keep it dark, for some folks makes themselves so nasty pertic'ler. White bulldog in corner whines in approval and, rushing to end of chain, places his chin against your knee. Thirsty customers produce dogs from most unexpected parts of their body and whisper enquiries as to fight and guv'nor's chances. The conversation is only momentarily interrupted and continues to revolve around dog fight, match and "Welsh Arp" up to the time you leave.*

Bill Tupper's Greyhound Inn was a very well known sporting drum and prior to the Cremorne show Bill Tupper owned both the Greyhound in Webber Row and the Boars Head in Long Acre. At the time of the Cremorne show, the Boars Head was not open to the public. Bill Tupper loved a wager and hated to lose an argument. The goading of James Hinks into risking everything by putting his reputation and that of his new "type" of bull terrier on the line whilst Bill Tupper risked nothing himself would be his kind of wager. Bill Tupper, due to his ownership of a sporting drum for many years did have access to dogs that were "bred to the business". What of the wager "£5 and a case of champagne", which at first sight seems brash. However, evidenced by the reports in Bells Life, Bill Tupper had no hesitation in laying wagers of £25 and £50, even paying the expenses of challengers from the provinces to bring their dogs to his sporting drum in London. So why only £5 on the Puss fight? Again, the intention would be to tempt and cajole James Hinks into commitment. James Hinks had been awarded a prize valued at £5 when Puss won her class at the show. An amount of £5 was nothing to Bill Tupper but on this occasion his prize was not money but the destruction of what he saw to be an upstart rival from the provinces. A match was made and the contest, held at Bill Tupper's Blue Boar's Head, Long Acre. Dog fighting was illegal and this would no doubt have been a very closed affair for those *in the know*. The doors would be barred, windows blocked up and every aperture closed. No person would be allowed to leave under any circumstances until the fight was over. A few rats would be on hand as decoys in the unlikely event that the Police intervened. The contest in the Blue Boar lasted around half an hour, with Puss killing the challenger. This put the stamp on Hinks's white bull terrier and its popularity, particularly as a show dog, was immediately secured.

Bells Life reported that, at the Blue Boar, there was a *grand pit* which was a *triumph of mechanical skill.* The Blue Boar was in the ownership of Bill Tupper from early February 1863, the Cremorne Show was in late March and the Blue Boar's official public opening was in April. We have no way of knowing if the *grand pit* had been constructed at the time of the Puss fight but, in any case, the Blue Boars Head, in Long Acre, was certainly available for such a private, illegal, rendezvous.

The grand mechanical pit at Tupper's Blue Boar's Head

Bill Tupper did, however, take care of Mr McDonald who could not compete with the Blue Boar's regular sporting entertainment so close to his own sporting drum in Long Acre. As reported in Bells Life 17th May 1863: *Long Acre Canine and All Fancy Establishment – Great success attends upon this noted sporting hostelrie, the secret being that the amusements are as varying as they are first rate. Great dog shows every fortnight, when animals unsurpassed are exhibited; stock dogs unequalled in London; all breeds for sale. Rats in galore. Pit free, always ready and trials at any time. Monday June 2, the great ratting sweepstakes, entrance free, rats for pounds, for a splendid tea and coffee service, to be seen at the bar. An early entrance is required. Mr W Tupper wishes to thank his Nottingham friends, Mr Collishaw especially. Thursday May 21, a meeting of the pigeon fancy to agree to rules for the great Champion Challenge Cup of 50 guineas. Visitors to the Derby should call at the Blue Boars Head in Long Acre, for comfort, sport or accommodation.*

Within eighteen months of Bill Tupper owning the Blue Boars Head in Long Acre in direct competition with Mr McDonald's sporting drum, as reported in the 2nd December 1864 edition of The London Gazette, Mr McDonald entered into an arrangement with his creditors and conveyed all his estate and effects to the brewery who had called in his debt. This was a smart move by Mr McDonald because it avoided the stigma of bankruptcy and enabled him, in a very short time, to enter business again as the landlord of the Cremorne Arms in Chelsea. He later reopened his Scotch Stores in Oxford Street.

> **NOTICE is hereby given, that by a Deed dated the 8th day of November, 1864, made between William McDonald, of No. 27, Long-acre, in the county of Middlesex, Licensed Victualler, and Edward Adams, of Castle-street, Long-acre, in the said county of Middlesex, Clerk to Messrs. Combe, Delafield, and Company, Brewers, the said William McDonald conveyed all his estate and effects to the said Edward Adams, absolutely, to be applied and administered for the benefit of the creditors of the said William McDonald, in like manner as if he had been duly adjudged a bankrupt; and notice is hereby further given, that the said deed was executed by the said William McDonald, on the day of the date thereof; that the place of abode of the said Edward Adams is No. 4, Harley-road, Adelaide-road, Saint John's Wood, in the county of Middlesex; and that the execution of the said deed by the said William McDonald and Edward Adams respectively, is attested by John Neate, of No. 27, Orchard-street, Portman-square, in the county of Middlesex, Solicitor, whose place of abode is No. 53, Belsize-park, Hampstead, in the said county of Middlesex.—Dated this 1st day of December, 1864.**

As for Bill Tupper, things also did not go too well for him. He became seriously ill and was forced to take on a partner at the Blue Boar, Charles Mansfield. Unfortunately, whilst Bill Tupper was convalescing in Ash, near Aldershot, Mr Mansfield invited all the main winners from the 1864 Cremorne show to the Blue Boar, to exhibit their winning dogs at the hostelerie during the day, followed up with none other than Jemmy Shaw presiding in the evening.

This resulted in James Hinks attending the Blue Boar with Kit, Madman, Puss and Young Puss. There is no corroboration that these turn of events led to the brake up of the Tupper/Mansfield partnership at the Blue Boar but, within a few months they had gone their separate ways, with Mansfield retaining the Blue Boar in his own name and Tupper buying back his original haunt, the Greyhound. Bill Tupper's illness returned, as reported in the 6th May 1865 issue of Bells Life: *W. Tupper's Great Dog Show – This much respected fancier is now himself again, having become convalescent from his late long and severe illness.* Bill Tupper's severe illness again returned and in October 1865, he passed away. His son, J Tupper of Ash, Aldershot, took over the Greyhound. It would appear that Mr Mansfield lacked Bill Tupper's business acumen. On his own he did not last long, selling the Blue Boar in 1867.

To tidy up a final point, what of James Jr's account that the fight took place in 1862. James Jr's account was written when he was around the age of 82 and, with probably failing memory, I do believe that he would have probably taken the date from Rawdon B Lee's account written some forty years beforehand.

The Early Shows 1863 (Paris) - 1867

It was said that many good dogs of all breeds at the Cremorne show were bought by dealers to send over to France, with the intention of selling them on for a profit at the first French dog show, held in the gardens of the Zoological Acclimatisation in the Bois de Boulogne, outside Paris 3rd to 10th May 1863. The French show was held under the auspices of the Societe imperiale zoologique d'acclamation and was a scientific event to gather together a complete collection of dogs in order to scientifically distinguish pure breeds. Unlike the English dog shows, the French show was not organised on an entrepreneurial basis, nor for the benefit of exhibitors, nor for spectators and the zoologique organisation were the judges, rather than breed experts. Some 250 of the 1000 exhibits were disqualified as not being good enough examples of their breed. Nevertheless, thousands of French spectators attended over the 7 days of the show which was a great success.

The copy of the catalogue for the show that I viewed does not contain a list of exhibitors and I have not been able to establish whether James Hinks sent over any Bulldogs or Bull Terriers for exhibition. The catalogue discloses that there were 22 Bulldogs (18 dogs and 4 bitches) entered and an amazing 78 Bull-Terriers (54 dogs and 24 bitches). The list of prize winners discloses that there were no English Bulldog or Bull Terrier exhibitors in the prize winners, all the winners in the Bulldog and Bull Terrier classes being Frenchmen. It was also said that the French newspapers complained that there was a disproportionately large number of ugly dwarf bulldogs in the exhibition. Mr McDonald did well though, winning silver medals for a second and a third place in class 28 with his Blenheim spaniels called Grace and Jenny and a second prize of 50 francs and a 5th prize bronze medal in class 7 for two smooth haired terriers, called Daisy and Duke.

Following the Paris dog show, Mr McDonald again called a meeting, as reported in Bells Life: *The Caledonian Hall will be opened this evening, May 17, for a meeting of the London fanciers and their friends, on which occasion the prizes received from the French Exhibition will be shown and the particulars of the arrangements and the injustices of the awards to the English exhibitors will be fully explained by Mr McDonald. Mr McDonald will also be prepared to answer all questions respecting the forthcoming Islington Exhibition, the second division of which will be under the management of W McDonald, when he hopes to give satisfaction to the exhibitors and also to the Islington Hall and with the great patronage already received, there is no doubt that this exhibition will be the most successful.*

The First Great International Dog Show was held at the Agricultural Hall in Islington, London, 25th to 30th May 1863. In keeping with the public meeting following the previous Islington show, Mr McDonald was appointed manager of the non sporting section of the show and to provide further comfort to exhibitors, Mr Brailsford, secretary of the Birmingham National Dog Show, together with his experienced staff of Birmingham keepers, had been engaged to take charge of the internal arrangements at Islington. In addition to that, the owners of the Agricultural Hall guaranteed payment of all the prizes. This was a great step forward *for the protection of gentlemen who patronise the canine race.*

In Bulldogs (over 20lbs) Lamphier's King Dick remained supreme, taking 1st, 2nd was Mr Molloy's Nelly [2697] and 3rd Mr Pike's Lord Nelson. In the under 20lbs class, 1st was Mr Orme's Violet and 2nd went to Mr F Else's Floss [2678] (bought from Bill Tupper). James Hinks was highly commended with Rose. In the Bull Terrier class (over 10lbs) 1st was Mr Kendrick's Dick [2732], 2nd Mr F White's Rose [2828]. James Hinks was relegated to 3rd with Puss [2821] (the KC Stud Book has Puss taking 2nd prize, but this appears to be incorrect) and 4th was Mr West's Nell. In the under 10lbs class, Mr McDonald took 1st with Daisy [2800], 2nd was Mr Graham with Beauty [2796], whilst 3rd was Mr Hughes with Nell. Bill Tupper's name did not appear in the cards for any breed at this important London show and, perhaps, this was a consequence of events following the Cremorne show at the end of March.

The Fourth Annual Exhibition of sporting and other dogs held at the Old Wharf in Birmingham in December 1863 still did not feature classes for Bull

Terriers. In Bulldogs, the sexes were separated and Mr Lamphier's King Dick still reigned taking 1st place, 2nd was Mr Pike's Lord Nelson. In bitches Mr Lamphier's Venom [2714] was 1st and James Hink's was 2nd with Rose [2709]. James Hinks was also in the cards in other breeds, taking a 3rd with his home bred Mastiff, Tiger [2844] born in 1862 (by Lord Byron's Tiger ex Duchess), a 1st with a home bred Dalmatian, Lady, born 1862 (by Spot ex Lady), 1st with a Smooth Haired Terrier called Lady and 3rd with a Toy Terrier, Fan. Mr McDonald was in the cards with a Skye Terrier, two Blenheim Spaniels, two King Charles Spaniels and a Maltese.

The Second Exhibition of sporting and other dogs held at Ashburnham Hall, Cremorne, Chelsea took place 18th to 23rd March 1864. In Bull Terriers (over 10lbs), James Hinks cleaned up, taking 1st with Madman [2740] born in 1862 (by Old Madman ex Old Puss), 2nd was Madman's litter sister, Puss [2822] and third was their mother, (Old) Puss [2821]. In Bull Terriers (under 10lbs) James Hinks was 3rd with Kit [2811] (by Old Madman ex John Smith's Lady), whilst 1st was taken by Mr Brown's Wallace [2794] and 2nd was Mr Burt's Nettle [2817]. In Bulldogs (large size) Mr Lamphier's King Dick would not be denied, taking 1st. Bill Tupper was 2nd with Gambler [2624]. In Bulldogs (small size), Bill Tupper was 1st with Brandy and the bitch he sold to Mr Else, Floss, was 2nd.

The Second International Dog Show held at the Agricultural Hall, Islington, London from 27th to 31st May 1864 repeated the Cremorne placings for Bull Terriers with Madman and his litter sister, Puss, taking 1st and 2nd and their mother, Old Puss being 3rd. In the under 10lbs class, Mr W McDonald took 1st with Daisy, Mr McKendrick was 2nd with Dandy [2727] and James Hinks was 3rd with Wafer [2793] born in 1863 (by Brown's Racket ex Sill). In Bulldogs (over 20lbs), 1st was again Lamphier's King Dick, 2nd Mr Lee's Kit [2683] and 3rd Mr Pike's Lord Nelson. In the under 20lbs class, Mr Orme won with Violet, 2nd was Mr Gifford's Myrtle [2694] and 3rd Mr Gaze's Rose [2708]. James Hinks was also 2nd in Dalmatians with Spot [2577], 2nd in White Smooth Haired Terriers with Lilly (by Prince ex Venus), 2nd with a Black and Tan Terrier called Lady and 3rd with a Blenheim Spaniel.

The National Exhibition of sporting and other dogs held at the Old Wharf in Birmingham in late November/early December 1864 saw Bull Terrier classes for the first time. It would appear that the organisers of the show did not really hold the bull terrier with any sort of regard, as reported in the Birmingham Daily Gazette: *We now come to the Bull Terriers, a new class this year. The committee have hitherto fought shy of having anything to do with these dogs but they are highly popular amongst the dog fancier and the result of a little pressure is that they are admitted at last. A capital start is made, no fewer than twenty eight being shown.* James Hinks took 1st with Madman [2740] and 2nd with Madman's mother, Old Puss [2821], 3rd went to Mr Walker's Puss [2822]. This was Madman's litter sister that James Hinks had previously shown and sold on to Mr Walker. The KC Stud Book tells us that this Puss was *also belonging to Mr T E Walker* and this would account for her sometimes being shown by James Hinks and sometimes by Mr Walker. James Hinks was also in the cards with a Greyhound that he had bought in from Mr Harrison called Dart [181] born in 1862 (by Haine's Chap ex Harrison's Fly) and a smooth Haired Terrier called Empress [3539]. Hinks had sold his Mastiff, Tiger [2844] to Mr Barker who was placed 3rd, whilst he was unplaced with a two year old Mastiff called Lion. He also showed a Bloodhound called Vengeance that was 3 years old, a Curly Coated Retriever called Carlo, aged eighteen months, a Newfoundland called Lion and a fifteen month old Black and Tan Terrier, called Ben. James Hinks and Mr McDonald were in the same classes with their King Charles Spaniels and Toy Terriers and Mr McDonald was in the cards with a Pug. In Bulldogs, the classes were split, Mr Lamphier's King Dick being 1st in the dogs, with Mr Pike's Nelson 2nd. In bitches, Mr Lamphier took 1st with Madge [2689], 2nd was Mr Reeve's Pansy [2702].

On 22nd December 1864, The Fourth Dog Show was held in the Zoological Gardens, Manchester. Whilst this was the Fourth show in Manchester, none of the first three were included in the KC Stud Book and no KC Stud Book entries were awarded to Bulldogs or Bull Terriers at this show either. In Bull Terriers, Mr Royds won best dog with his Madman [2750] and James Hinks took best bitch with Puss.

Royds Madman gave rise to another great Bull Terrier fable, Mr Royds was a well known breeder and exhibitor of British birds, tumbler pigeons, poultry and foreign finches and, the story goes, must have thought that he had got off to a great start with his first Bull Terrier by buying the famous Madman. Royds Madman [2750] was bred by James Hinks and was, in fact, the litter brother to Hinks' famous Madman [2740]. The fable tells us that Mr Royds believed he had bought Hinks' famous Madman. In the catalogue for the sixth Birmingham Show in 1865, Mr Royds gave detailed breeding of his Madman and placed a valuation on the dog of £100,000. The fable relates that this valuation was said to emphasise that his was the famous Madman. At the Manchester Show in 1865, James Hinks was exhibiting the famous Madman [2740] in the same class as Royds Madman [2750]. James Hinks was first and Royds Madman was placed fourth.

Some breed history books also relate a story that in the mid 1860's a Mr Roberts became owner of the famous Madman and Mr Roberts and Mr Royds had spats as to which dog was the real famous Madman. At one show where they both exhibited, it was claimed that one of them actually swapped over the prize cards. At least one breed history book relates that on occasion Royds Madman was placed over Hinks's famous Madman. Again, research has shown the truth of the matter, that being the Old Madman/Puss litter actually contained three litter brothers all called Madman. James Hinks owned the famous Madman and both Mr Royds and Mr Roberts owned litter brothers also called Madman. This can be verified by the fact that, at the Fifth Birmingham Show in 1864, the Alexandra Park show in 1864 and at Islington in June 1865, James Hinks and Mr Roberts both exhibited their respective Madman litter brothers in the same class!

So what of Mr Royds valuation of £100,000, purportedly said to emphasise that his was the famous Madman. This is also put into context by the fact that Mr Royds also exhibited a Pug at the Birmingham Show in 1865, called Moscow, on which he also placed a valuation of £100,000. Exhibitors had to place a suggested purchase price in the catalogue for their exhibit and sometimes dogs changed ownership once or twice before the show ended. By placing a valuation of £100,000 on his Bull Terrier and his Pug, it appears that Mr Royds was simply ensuring that no one would meet his valuation and he could take his dogs home with him, good for him.

The Third Great International Dog Show held at the Agricultural Hall, Islington, London took place 2nd to 6th June 1865. In Bull Terriers, James Hinks took 1st and 2nd with Madman [2740] and Old Puss [2821], 3rd was Mr Whyman with Bobby. Mr Roberts gained a highly commended with his Madman as did James Hinks with Nettle. In Bull Terriers under 10lbs, Mr Ferriman took second place with Wafer, standing behind Mr Newman's Dandy. In Bulldogs over 20lbs, King Dick was again 1st, 2nd was Mr Brown's

Saxon [2648], 3rd Mr H Brown's Cribb [2601]. Under 20lbs, 1st withheld, 2nd Mr Higg's Cribb [2604]. James Hinks was also in the cards with a White Smooth Haired Terrier, Fly [3544], a Scotch Terrier and a Toy.

December 1865 saw the Sixth Great Annual Exhibition of sporting and other dogs, held at Curzon Hall, Birmingham. In Bulldog bitches, James Hinks was 1st with Rush [2711], 2nd Mr Reeve's Pansy. King Dick won the Champion class and Mr Price's Romanie [2644] the Open class. In Bull Terriers (large size, over 15lbs) 1st was Mr Boyce's Tartar [2777], bred by James Hinks and born in 1864 (by Turk ex Old Puss), 2nd was Mr Royd's Madman [2750]. James Hinks also gained a highly commended with Old Puss, now aged 4 years and three months. In small size Bull Terriers, 1st was Mr Willock's Billy [2722] and 2nd Mr Boyce's Dick. James Hinks was also in the cards with the Smooth Haired Terrier, Fly [3544], a Dandie Dinmont, a Pug and a Toy Terrier.

Prior to the fifth Manchester Dog Show in the Zoological Gardens, on 22nd December 1865, interest in the Bulldog classes had been stimulated by a challenge issued in Bells Life from Mr Berdetta to Mr Thomas. This may have come about because Mr Berdetta was German and his dog was referred to disparagingly as "the German's dog": *D Berdetta will show his bulldog Brilliant against E Thomas's bulldog Gambler for £5 or £10 a side, each to pick a judge and the Editor of Bells Life to choose the umpire. The Editor of Bells Life to be the stakeholder. A reply through this paper will be attended to.* Mr Thomas's reply was short and to the point: *E Thomas is surprised at Mr Berdetta's challenge as Mr B knows that if he will go to Manchester and put any money down that ET's bulldog shall show against Mr B's bulldog, for any amount from £10 up to £100. The match can be made by sending any part of that sum to Bellvue, to show at the present dog show.*

In the over 12lbs Bulldog class, Mr Thomas settled the challenge and won the class with Gambler [2623], 2nd was Mr Berdetta's Brilliant [2597] and 3rd Mr Price's Romanie. In Bulldogs under 12lbs, James Hinks took 1st with Nell [2696] (by Frank ex Lilly), 2nd was Mr Hill's Cherry. Classes in Bull Terriers were split between the sexes, in dogs James Hinks was 1st with Madman [2740], 2nd Mr Walker's Spring [2744], 3rd Mr Phillips Danger [2728] and bringing up the rear in 4th was Mr Royds Madman [2750]. In bitches, James Hinks was 1st with Puss [2822] and 2nd was Mr Guest's Wasp [2832]. Hinks was also in the cards gaining 2nd with his Greyhound, Dart [181], a 1st with his Bloodhound bitch, Vengeance and a 1st with the Pug, Topsy. Awards at this show finally achieved KC Stud Book recognition.

Easter 1866 saw the death of two great bulldog characters, they being Mr Lamphier and his great dog King Dick, as reported in the Birmingham Gazette: *DEATH OF THE CHAMPION BULLDOG – The well known champion bulldog, King Dick, has paid the debt of nature under rather peculiar circumstances. On Easter Tuesday Mr Lamphier of Handworth, the owner of the dog, died. After that event Dick exhibited the most profound grief for the loss of his master. He would not rest anywhere except on the chair upon which his master used to sit and whenever he could get into the room in which he died he gave expression to his feelings in the most vehement howling, broken by low growls and other vocal signs of sorrow. He refused his food and on Sunday week he followed his master. In fact the faithful animal may be said to have died of grief.*

The first week in December 1866 saw the Seventh Great Annual Exhibition of sporting and other dogs, held at Curzon Hall, Birmingham. In Bull Terriers (large size), James Hinks was 1st with Rebel [2767], born in 1863 (by Old Madman ex Old Puss) and 2nd with Puss [2821]. In small size Bull Terriers, James Hinks again took 1st and 2nd with Dick [2730] and Daisy [2801] born in 1864 (by Turk ex Old Daisy). Whilst Daisy was home bred, Dick, born in 1865 had been bought in. Dick was by Old Dazzler out of Richard's Lady (Lady by Glass's Dudley ex J Tailby's Nothing, said to be a well known fighting dog in Birmingham). In Bulldogs, 1st Mr Reeve's Cure [2609], 2nd Mr Henshall's Gambler [2623], previously owned by Mr Thomas. In bitches, 1st went to Mr Whitehouse's Rush [2711], which Mr Whitehouse had bought from James Hinks, 2nd was Mr Guymer's Polly [2703] (by Lord Nelson [2637], once owned by James Hinks, out of Holland's Kit, Kit by Carey's Charlie ex Carey's Nettle). Holland's Kit was therefore a half sister to Holland's Poll, the mother of Hink's bulldog bitch Madman [2690]. James Hinks was also in the cards with his Smooth Haired Terrier and the Pug, Topsy.

Manchester's Sixth Show at the Zoological Gardens followed, towards the end of December 1866. In Bull Terrier dogs, 1st was James Hinks with Madman [2740], 2nd Mr Royds Madman [2750], 3rd Hinks's Rebel [2767]. In bitches, James Hinks was 1st with Puss [2822] and 2nd was Mr Wright with Lill. James

Hinks was also in the cards with Fly, his English Terrier. Over 12lbs Bulldogs went to Mr Thomas's Gambler [2623], 2nd was Mr Berdetta's Brilliant [2597] and 3rd Mr Leitch's Jock. In the under 12lbs Bulldogs class, James Hinks took 1st with Nell [2696].

The Eighth Great Annual Exhibition of sporting and other dogs was held at Curzon Hall, Birmingham in the first week in December 1867. In Bull Terriers (large size, over 15lbs), James Hinks was 1st with Young Puss [2823] born 1865 (by Madman ex Puss), 2nd was Rev Mellor's Danger [2728]. In small size Bull Terriers, 1st was Mr Swann's Dick [2730]. Mr Swann had bought Dick from James Hinks. Dick was also to be owned by Mr Godfree, prior to going to Mr S E Shirley, one of the founders of the Kennel Club and a keen Bulldog and Bull Terrier man. 2nd was Mr Swan's Nelson [2758] born in 1866 and bred by one of Hinks's associates, Mr Willocks (by Stokes's, previously Potter's, Bill out of Willock's Julia). Again, this dog would be owned by another of James Hinks's associates, Mr Godfree, prior to being crowned a champion under the ownership of Mr Shirley. In Bulldogs, 1st was Mr Butler's Stead [2650], 2nd Mr Gloster's Little Dick [2636] (whose dam was Slut, by Hinks's Jerry ex Bagnall's Slut) Jerry was described as being white, with tulip ears and a frog mouth. Whilst a protruding jaw was a point insisted on by old time breeders, it looked very unsightly on the show bench. There was therefore a grudging countenance of frog mouthed dogs, that being Bulldogs with wide but level jaws, rather than undershot. Little Dick had been disqualified at a show in Hanley for faked ears. Faking Bulldog ears was a process where the ear sinews were cut, Bulldogs were also faked by cutting the sinews of the upper lips. 3rd was Mr Lawrence's Romeo [2645] who was litter brother to Little Dick. In Bulldog bitches, 1st was Mr Mr Nichol's with Beauty [2664] and 2nd Mr Lamphier's son with Meg [2692] (by King Dick ex Old Nell). James Hinks was also in the cards with his Bloodhound, Empress. He also exhibited an over 65lb Pointer called Ranger, born in 1865. Nice to see Mr McDonald back in the fold, taking 2nd with his Italian Greyhound, Duke.

The Seventh Manchester Show at the Zoological Gardens was in December 1867. In Bull Terrier dogs James Hinks took 2nd, 3rd and 4th with Young Rebel [2768] born in 1866 (by Rebel [2767] ex Kit), Young Madman [2745] born 1866 (by Old Madman ex Puss) and Turk [2782] born 1866 (by Rebel ex Fly). They stood behind Mr Butler's Charlie [2723]. In bitches James Hinks took 1st and 2nd with Young Puss [2823] born 1865 (by Madman ex Puss) and Wasp [2833] born 1866 (by Old Turk ex Nettle). In Bulldogs, 1st was Mr Wright's King Dick [2634], 2nd Mr Barber's King Dick [2632], 3rd Mr Robson's Saxon [2648]. In bitches, Mr Eden was 1st with Juno [2682] and Mr Nichols 2nd with Beauty [2664].

Old Victor and Young Victor

It is not so clear whether James Hinks used a Greyhound or Greyhound cross as a surreptitious back cross. Such conjecture being stimulated by the appearance in the show ring, in 1868, of Victor [2791] (later known as Old Victor). J H Walsh (Stonehenge) in Dogs of the British Isles, described Old Victor: *At that time there was still a slight reminder of the bull in the comparatively full lip but in 1868 Old Victor suddenly appeared from the Black Country without this appendage and with such a fine form of head and frame that he succeeded in gaining the fiats of the judges in his favour; and his type has since then been installed as that which is to be considered the proper one for the breed. Nothing is known of his pedigree and all the guesses at his greyhound parentage are purely hypothetical. He was, like all the "Madmen" of Mr Hinks' breeding a pure white.....*

Old Victor, whilst being ahead of the Bull Terriers that went before him, in that he was not only more refined in body but also much less lippy than his forebears with good length of foreface, was owned by James Hinks, was said variously to have been bred by him, was said to be of "pedigree unknown" and, as related by J H Walsh, it was also muted that Old Victor's refinement was down to some Greyhound blood behind him. The Greyhound (if James Hinks did in fact use one) would no doubt have been white. That is not to say that Old Victor's sire or dam was a white Greyhound, the Greyhound blood, if it ever was, would have been introduced by a back crossing programme going back at least three or four generations until the Greyhound genes not required were bred out whilst those being desired were retained. The progeny carrying the undesirable genes being vigorously destroyed/discarded or perhaps sold as sporting greyhounds for poaching and those still in the back crossing programme being kept out of public view.

The first KC Stud book shows that James Hinks only owned and only showed one Greyhound that was in the cards. This was a dog that he bought in from a Mr Harrison, called Dart and which was born in 1862. Unfortunately, the KC Stud Book does not give the colour of Dart. However, James Hinks did breed a greyhound litter sired by Dart, as he won a second prize at Crewe in 1870 with his son also, of course, called Dart (by Old Dart out of Fly). The surreptitious use of Dart as a back cross would not only provide great refining quality but also help in providing a naturally close, thin, coat. James Hinks owned Old Victor, however, strange as it may seem, there does not appear to be any evidence from the KC Stud Books or show catalogues that I have seen, that James Hinks used Old Victor at stud or even showed the dog. This would perhaps indicate that Old Victor was just a puppy when he was in the hands of James Hinks. Old Victor's age was not known because he was of "pedigree unknown". Old Victor first appeared in the show ring in 1868, only after James Hinks had sold him as part of a kennel clear out.

Bull Terriers appeared to change hands at an amazing rate, some having 4 or 5 different owners during their lifetime. In fact, James Hinks appears to have had a good clear out of his stock on more than one occasion. During 1868 and 1869 he sold a good part of his kennel to Mr J H Ryder of Old Trafford, Manchester. After a short time, Mr Ryder sold the dogs on to Mr George Smith of Timperley in Cheshire who also showed them successfully, with Old Victor being later sold by Mr Smith to Mr Chorley of Kendal. Old Victor's age was not known because he was of "pedigree unknown". He died in 1872, having been found by none other than Rawden B Lee, smothered in his box at the Crystal Palace Show. Apparently, there appeared to be nothing suspicious about his death. Old Victor was said to be of unsound temperament and remained so until in the hands of Mr Chorley who affected somewhat of a cure by supplying Old Victor with copious amounts of beer to drink.

Mr Smith did place Old Victor at stud and his progeny took the breed by storm. Mr Mayhew, a Birmingham breeder and an associate of James Hinks, used Old Victor on a bitch that he obtained from another associate of James Hinks, Mr Willock. The bitch was called Features and was not only also of "pedigree unknown" but interestingly was also said to be a bitch *well known for her great length of foreface.* So, here we have a dog, Old Victor, of "pedigree unknown" mated to a bitch, Features, of "pedigree unknown" or, were the pedigrees of these dogs "known" to James Hinks and his close associates but kept secret because they involved, perhaps, a past generations dalliance with a Greyhound (we will never know). This mating produced a good dog called Victor [2789] (known as Mayhew's Victor) who, as noted below, took first prize at Manchester in December 1870.

Mr Steele mated his home bred "Puss" (by Old Victor ex Old Puss) at her first season to Mayhew's Victor and this half brother half sister mating produced one heck of a litter. The litter was born around September 1870 and James Hinks and his close associates bought up the whole litter. The litter included Prince [2760] (known as White Prince) who was owned by James Hinks and then Fred Hinks; Rebel [2769] also owned by Fred Hinks; whilst Puss [2819], Venom [2830], Young Rebel and Young Victor [2792] were bought by Mr Godfree. Mr Godfree later sold Puss [2819] to Mr Tredinnick who showed her with success.

Young Victor [2792], otherwise known as "the patched" or "mark eyed dog" was variously owned by Mr Steel (who bred him), Mr G Smith (who owned his grandsire, Old Victor), Mr J Willock of Bimingham (who owned his grandmother, Features) Mr Moore of Manchester (who campaigned him under the name of Madman II), Mr Godfree of Birmingham and finally Mr Pfeil of Surrey. Now this mark eyed dog caused much controversy at the time, not only because both his parents were pure white, but he transcended white and coloured classes by cheekily being entered and winning both classes for white dogs and also classes restricted to coloureds. That would have certainly rubbed some people up the wrong way and it did. These controversies were to be his downfall as, after he won a first prize at Hull in 1875, Young Victor was found dead – poisoned on his show bench.

Young Victor from a woodcut by Ludlow

Young Victor was also the sire, amongst others, of the great Tarquin [2776] born in 1873 out of Puss (by Hinks' Gambler [2737] out of Young Puss). Tarquin was bred by Mr C L Boyce.

of Birmingham and later owned by the venerable Mr Vero Shaw. Vero Shaw also bought in from Mr Godfree a half sister of Tarquin, sired by Young Victor out of Godfree's Puss. This bitch was shown by Mr Godfree under the name of Glare but Vero Shaw changed her name and exhibited her under the name of "Slaughter". Not long after James Hinks' death, Mr Godfree was to sell the rest of his kennel to Vero Shaw.

James Hinks withdraws from Show Scene

It has been variously written and repeated by the conformists in many breed books that James Hinks withdrew from the public show scene in 1870. The writers' then shrug their shoulders and move on, leaving the reader none the wiser.

It took very little research time to discover that this statement was not factually correct, because although James Hinks withdrew from the Bull Terrier show scene during 1870, he did exhibit four different dog breeds at the Birmingham Show in December 1870. He then appeared to stay away from all dog shows during 1871, with the exception of the last show of that year, being Manchester in late December 1871, when he really had something to shout about. He also continued to exhibit his Bulldogs and the occasional Bull Terrier until selling his Bull Terriers to Mr Hartley in 1874. He carried on breeding bull terriers after that date.

So, why did he withdraw from the public show scene during 1870 and 1871. Research indicates that there may be three reasons for this withdrawal that can be substantiated. The first two were serious reputational issues that would affect the way that right minded people would feel, think and act towards him when they saw him at dog shows and the third issue appears to have been poor judgement during a kennel clear out, leaving him with inferior show stock, compared with the dogs he had sold. Now, it is not possible to say with any certainty that these were the cause of his withdrawal from showing but they may well have had some great influence on the matter. So let us look at these matters in detail and, as with the Puss fight, readers can form their own views on these matters.

The first reputational issue was a serious incident and Court case involving James Hinks in January 1870. Following this Court case and a further Court case shortly after in March, it appears that James Hinks did not exhibit at dog show for the rest of 1870. He did, however, exhibit his Bulldog Crib, a Black and Tan Terrier, a Toy Terrier and a French Night Dog at the Birmingham show in December of that year. He may have exhibited these breeds to test public reaction to his reappearance. Perhaps he received short shrift because he then did not exhibit at dog shows during the greater part of 1871.

James Hinks was hauled before the Longton Police Court, charged with "unlawfully, wantonly and maliciously maiming and wounding a dog". I had previously read that this case was "dropped". The phrase "dropped" means that the charge was not proceeded with. However, that was not factually correct. James Hinks was charged with the offence and the case was heard in Court. If the incident, the two Court cases and the general fallout that followed the publication of the matters caused or was a factor in causing James Hinks to withdraw from the public life of dog showing, then it is has great historical significance. Reports of the cruelty case appeared in the local papers and the Staffordshire Sentinel. A full report of the court case appeared in the Birmingham Daily Post on 20th January 1870 and is restated here for the benefit of readers who can make up their own minds as to its significance:

The Birmingham Daily Post.

VOL. XVI. No. 3,590. BIRMINGHAM, THURSDAY, JANUARY 20, 1870. PRICE ONE PENNY.

CHARGE OF CRUELTY AGAINST BIRMINGHAM DOG FANCIER

At the Longton Police Court yesterday, James Hinks, of Worcester Street, Birmingham, was charged with unlawfully, wantonly and maliciously maiming and wounding a dog, of the value of £20, the property of John William Nichols, grocer, Newcastle Under Lyme. Mr A Tennant on behalf of the prosecution, said the cruelty complained of took place at the recent dog show at Hanley. Both the complainant and the defendant were exhibitors of bull-terriers and it is suggested that the superiority of the complainant's dog was the reason of the defendant's cruelty, in order to prevent it from getting a prize. Instead of getting a prize, the complainant's dog had to be attended by a veterinary surgeon and sent home wounded and sick. It had been cruelly beaten by the defendant, who was seen by several witnesses to beat the animal in a most unmerciful manner, to seize it by the neck and beat it with his clenched fist as hard as he could on the head and, not satisfied with that, he caught up the dog by the skin of its neck and nearly throttled it, after which he held it down with his left hand and beat it with the buckle end of a dog collar about the face; then held it up by the tail and again beat it unmercifully. His excuse was that the dog was fighting with his own, which was in the next stall; but there was abundant evidence to show that his ill treatment of the dog was wanton and unprovoked. Mr Hinks was not a poor man, or a man who did not know better. The complainant, Mr Nicholas, said he exhibited two dogs at the Hanley show, one of them a white bull-and-terrier which he considered very valuable. He left this dog about eight in the evening of the day before the show opened. On Wednesday, the dog was brought back to him at Newcastle in a sad condition. Its throat hung four or five inches in a congealed state. The jaw was bruised and cut and the upper lip was split in two places. Its mouth could scarcely be opened with main force and it could not take its food. The damage done to the dog was estimated at £3, – the defendant said the dog was ticketed "dangerous" in the show and produced a letter from the hon. sec. confirming that statement. The complainant said he had the tickets put up only to keep people from going near the dog, because it was excited on account of his (complainant) leaving it. The defendant said when he went to fasten his dog next to the complainant's dog, the latter bounced at him. He directly put out his hand and threw it away, in doing so the dog bit his hand. He denied beating the dog and said its collar would cause the swelling spoken of, by straining, – Walter Sheppard, publican, Mill Street, Hanley, said he took a dog to the show on the Monday night, when he saw Hinks catch hold of complainant's dog by the collar and beat it with his clenched fist on the head. He then took a collar out of his pocket and beat the dog with the buckle-end, pinning it down and beating it about the nose and mouth. He beat the dog very severely. It was doing nothing to provoke this. The defendant denied this statement generally, – John Plant, another exhibitor, Mr Turfford, superintendant of dogs; Mr Hodgkins, veterinary surgeon, Newcastle, also gave evidence, the first two more or less corroborating the previous witnesses. In reply to Mr Davis, they said the defendant did not beat the dog clandestinely but openly and a number of persons were within a short distance. He seemed to be in a passion. Plant said complainant's dog was not so good as defendant's and could not have taken the prize from the latter if it had been quite well. Mr Llewellyn said the dog was brought to him on Wednesday, when he found a large lump in the neck, the result of force. The lower jaw was discoloured which must have been caused by violence; and the cut on the lip must have been produced by a sharp instrument. After hearing the witnesses for the complainant, Mr Davis said the charge could not be supported. The charge was unlawfully and maliciously maiming and wounding the dog. The dog was wounded and it may have been done unlawfully, but the case failed in the essential ingredient in the statute that it was done maliciously. If it had been shown that it had been done with malice, no punishment would have been too severe for such an act of atrocity. The charge was dismissed.

Some may say that James Hinks got off the charge on a technicality, he did wound the dog, it was an unlawful wounding but because, under the exact wording of the legislation, he did not plan intentionally to do it (maliciously) he got away with it. The legal definition of malicious being "with harmful intent" (ie malice aforethought). Others may say that the charge was correctly dismissed, the action by James Hinks being taken in the heat of the moment, *he seemed to be in a passion,* because Nichols's dog had first gone for his own and then, when James Hinks intervened, the dog bit him on the hand.

However, there could have been another reason that contributed to James Hinks being so short on temper that day, that being finding two other familiar dogs benched by Mr George Smith (which were to take the main prizes in large bull terrier dogs and bull terrier bitches). As related in the third reason for his withdrawal, below, he had sold his best dogs to Mr Ryder, who had sold them on to Mr Smith and he now found them benched at a small show in his own back yard!

Either way, the incident, the Court case and its wide reporting thereof in the local press would have had some detrimental effect on him personally and his reputation – and it did because James Hinks had cause to write to the Birmingham Daily Gazette: *Sir – in last Friday's Gazette, appears a paragraph headed "Charge of cruelty by Birmingham dog fancier."......the same if uncontradicted would prove of serious consequence to me in my business.*

The second serious reputational issue came very shortly after, in March 1870, when, at a Court case in Ashton, James Hinks was named as one of the central figures in an international dog stealing fraternity. This followed on from the Crewe Show of Dogs, Poultry and Rabbits in February, at which James Hinks and a Mr Isaac Watt Boulton were both exhibiting. Not long after the show, Mr Boulton's dog was stolen. At the Court case where a Mr Francis Smith was cleared of personally stealing the dog but was found guilty of purchasing the dog knowing it to have been stolen, Smith clearly named James Hinks as the recipient of the stolen dog and it was James Hinks who very quickly sent the dog on to Paris via London, Newhaven and Dieppe to his associate, Mr Bult, a fellow dog dealer. We have to thank the Ashton Weekly Reporter for their report on the Court case, which went into some detail about dog stealing and Mr Boulton's extraordinary efforts to be reunited with his stolen dog:

The Ashton Reporter.

CIRCULATING IN ASHTON-UNDER-LYNE, STALYBRIDGE, GLOSSOP, DUKINFIELD, MOSSLEY, HYDE, MOTTRAM, GORTON, OPENSHAW, DROYLSDEN, DENTON, HOOLEY HILL, AUDENSHAW, WATERLOO, BARDSLEY, LEES, HURST, &c., &c.

SATURDAY, MARCH 12, 1870. PRICE—THREE HALF PENCE

Public Notices. Business Notices.

FROM ASHTON TO LONDON AND PARIS IN SEARCH OF A DOG

On 17th of last month, a dog belonging to Mr Isaac Watt Boulton, engineer, Ashton, mysteriously disappeared. It was not a tiny animal which a thief could pick up and pocket or bag, but a fine noble looking dog of the Mount St Bernard and mastiff breed, some 22 months old, weighing over 175lbs and bearing the appropriate title of "Nero". On the 25th January, Nero was showing off his figure at the dog show at Crewe and it is believed that the fraternity of dog stealers, which is evidently a very numerous and select body, spotted Nero there and determined on having him. It is a well known fact that these dog thieves are a thoroughly organised body, expert at getting hold of all dogs worth having and, by a sort of underground railway plan transmitting them from one town to another until finally disposed of in England or France.

A day or two after Nero's disappearance, Mr Boulton issued reward bills and the Chief Constable sent copies to the various police offices in the country. On the 28th February, the Chief Constable received an intimation from the

Birmingham police that a dog answering the description of Nero arrived at the Birmingham railway station on the morning of the 18th February. It had been put on the railway at Longsight station, Manchester and was consigned to a respectable man named Hinks, a dog dealer, Worcester Street, Birmingham. The police sent another note, stating that the same dog had been dispatched by rail on the 21st February to Kensington Station, London. Having obtained this information, Mr Boulton, on Tuesday week, saw the station master at Longsight and, from what that gentleman said, he was satisfied that the dog which had thus been sent on to Birmingham and thence to London was his property. The man who had sent it from Longsight was called Smith of Gorton Brook, afterwards apprehended, who was in the habit of sending dogs to different parts of the country in that way. Next day Mr Boulton, being resolved on having his dog back set off to London in search of it. He made enquiries in Kensington, Hammersmith etc and at length was informed that a dog similar to the one described had been sent to Paris via Newhaven and Dieppe, on the night of the 21st February, being consigned to a man named Bult.

Mr Boulton set off to Paris at once starting at half past seven in the evening, Thursday. He arrived in Paris, via Dover and Calais, at seven o'clock on the Friday morning. The London police had furnished him with the name and address of a Paris detective but the detective being out of the way, he engaged an interpreter, who turned out a "duffer" and so he turned his steps to the British Embassy. After stating his case, Lord Cowley's secretary gave Mr Boulton a letter of introduction to the Prefect of Police and that functionary gave him the assistance of two detectives. One of them went at once to the railway station and get the address of Bult, which was R. Bult, 74 Avenue de la Grand Armee, Paris. They then drove off to that place and Mr Boulton and one of the detectives were admitted into the house by Mrs Bult. They wanted, they said, to buy a large dog. There was a very large number of dogs in the house and on the premises in the rear of the dwelling but, as they were passing a room leading to the back, Mr Boulton noticed the woman close the door hastily and in such a way as to excite suspicion. After going over the house without seeing the object of his search, he was determined to have a peep in to the room where he had seen the suspicious circumstance mentioned above. The woman said there was nothing particular in it "only a small pony." Mr Boulton said he should like to see it and getting further evasive answers, he declared that he would see it and at once commenced to remove a lot of lumber that had been reared against the door since he had entered the building. Having cleared that away, he opened the door, when Nero sprang out upon him and gave him such a greeting as to leave no doubt on the minds of those present as to whose dog it was.

Bult was away in England, having gone to Oxford and his wife saying that he would doubtless be with Hinks at Birmingham at that very time. Mr Boulton found that he had no power to take the dog away unless he paid the £20 which Bult had given Hinks for the dog and he telegraphed to the Birmingham police desiring them to tell Hinks that he had discovered the dog, that he awaited the receipt of £20 to regain possession of it and that he would see Hinks about his own expenses on his return from London. He also telegraphed to Mr Dalgleish, Chief Constable, and that official at once had Smith apprehended. Next morning, Mr Boulton went again to Bult's, when he saw a telegram saying "Let Mr Boulton have the dog free of any charge." He left Paris for home with the dog at four o'clock on Saturday morning last and reached Ashton by about eleven o'clock on Sunday night. Nero was regarded as a dog of considerable value in Paris, Bult having refused 3,000 francs, or £120 for it and it was entered for a great show to be held in that city on the 24th instant.

Mr Boulton has done good service to the public in thus indirectly exposing the system of dog stealing going on amongst us. As Mr Lord very properly expressed it in the Borough Court on Thursday, no gentleman can keep a dog worth having for any length of time but we hope the conviction of Smith will have a salutary effect on the thieves in future.

The case came before the Ashton Borough Court on Monday, when Francis Smith, dog dealer, Western Gorton, near Manchester was charged with stealing Nero on 17th February. The following evidence was given: Mr Isaac Watt Boulton, engine builder, Ashton said the large Mount St Bernard dog in Court is my property and I last saw it safe about two o'clock on the afternoon of the 17th February. About nine o'clock next morning I was informed by the man who fed the dog that he was missing. I acquainted the police with the fact and inquiries were made and from information

Mr Dalgleish, the Chief Constable gave to me I went to the Longsight railway station and from what the station master said to me I went to London on Wednesday night. I called upon the police there and ultimately I got to Kensington station. I found that my dog had arrived there in the afternoon of the 21st February. I made further inquiries and learned that the dog had been taken to Paris. I resolved to follow him to France and left London on Thursday night arriving in Paris on Friday morning. I went to the English Embassy there and got an introduction to the French detective police and I ultimately found the dog in the Champ d'Elysees, in the charge of an Englishman who dealt in dogs and who had some 50 or 60 dogs in his possession. I found that the Paris police could not compel the dog to be given up unless the £20 which he had paid for the dog was returned. The dog keeper himself was in England, he having left Paris for Oxford on the Wednesday and I was told was in all likelihood at Hinks' in Birmingham. I telegraphed to Mr Dalgleish and he communicated with Hinks at Birmingham. Ultimately the Paris police took the matter in hand and brought a magistrate on the dog dealer's premises and the woman was bound to appear before the magistrates. On the Saturday morning, when I went to her she had received a telegram from her husband at Birmingham to give me the dog and I brought him with me. There were some 50 or 60 dogs in the place and I fancy I know there were some very valuable dogs that had been stolen from this neighbourhood and from Manchester. About five weeks ago I exhibited at a dog show at Crewe and Hinks of Birmingham was also an exhibitor at the same show.

Thomas Outerside said: I am the station master at Longsight station, near Manchester. On the 17th February the prisoner (Smith) brought the dog produced to our station and consigned it by the 10:30 train at night to a man named Hinks, Worcester Street, Birmingham. He has consigned dogs to Hinks before and he sent dogs to all parts from time to time. Hinks I know is a dog dealer, for I have been in his shop and have seen 50 or 60 dogs there.

Prisoner: Oh, I certainly consigned the dogs to Hinks.

Sergeant Bolton said: About three o'clock on Saturday morning he and Sergeant Appleyard of the Manchester County Police stationed at Gorton went to the prisoner's house at West Gorton with a warrant for his apprehension. We knocked at the door and in a while, the prisoner's wife appeared at the window. I asked her to come down and open the door. She said "what for?" I told her I wanted her husband. She said "He very seldom sleeps at home, he is not at home now." She refused to come down and Sergeant Appleyard told her we held a warrant for his apprehension and that if she did not open the door we should be compelled to break it open, for we must be satisfied whether he was at home or not. She closed the window and went in the room. We waited about three quarters of an hour but receiving no answer in that time, we broke open the door, went upstairs and found that the prisoner had just got out of bed and was partially dressed......When I was searching the house, he asked me what I was looking for. I said I was looking for letters, whereupon Mrs Smith went downstairs and Sergeant Appleyard detected her in the act of attempting to destroy a number of letters....... Two letters were amongst the number and read as follows:

Birmingham, 25th February 1870. Mr Smith – Dear sir – Mr Inks is from home for a few days and you had better not send any more dogs until his return on Monday, of which he will write you – yours truly, J. HINKS

Birmingham, March 2nd 1870. Mr Smith – Dear sir – The retriever is not class good enough for me, so I must return him but if the mastiff is a good one and the deerhound you wrote about is a good one, send the two and the pugs, by the first train after you get this and I will give you a fair price for them. – Yours truly, J HINKS

Smith denied stealing the dog, saying that he had bought it off two men that approached him, for £2.10 shillings. After reviewing the evidence the learned advocate asked the bench to visit this case with the £20 penalty and the maximum six months alternative hard labour and as for Hinks, perhaps he would be dealt with at Birmingham.

The bench having consulted the Chairman said they had fully considered this case and they were of opinion that it was a very clear one and a very serious one too. They had no doubt prisoner had purchased the dog knowing it to have been stolen, for the very sum of the dog ought to have been convinced that £2.10 shillings was not a price that would be taken for such an animal that had been honestly come by. The bench had therefore come to the conclusion to inflict the full penalty of £20, or an alternative of four months imprisonment with hard labour.

At the conclusion of the case, Mr Dalgleish stated that there was another case of a spotted carriage dog having been stolen and consigned by Smith to Hinks on the 24th of last month, but as the owner did not care to prosecute if he got his dog returned, he did not purpose entering upon the case.

Whilst the details of the case were reported in Birmingham newspapers, it does not appear that any action was taken by the police, probably because it would not be able to be proven that James Hinks knew that the dogs consigned to him had been stolen. Nevertheless, word in the dog show scene would surely spread and being associated with dog stealers would make Hinks, in the eyes of many, "damned by association" and may have affected the way that dog show exhibitors would react towards him, particularly if they had previously had dogs stolen.

The third reason that can be substantiated for his withdrawal from the Bull Terrier show scene was that, in 1868/1869, he had sold all his best dogs to Mr Ryder (who showed them for a while and then sold them on to Mr G Smith) and, as the following show results evidence, the latest young Bull Terriers that James Hinks brought out could not compete with the ones he had sold. The dogs sold to Mr Ryder included the inevitably named Madman [2749], Puss [2823] (by Madman ex Puss), Daisy [2804] (by Rebel ex Puss), Rebel [2770] (by Old Madman ex Old Puss) and also the key dog referred to above, Old Victor [2791].

No sooner had James Hinks parted with his kennel to Mr Ryder, than he came out with another Madman [2741] (by Rebel ex Daisy). However, he did not then have things all his own way. At Manchester in late December 1868, James Hinks was placed third with Young Madman [2741] and fourth with Gambler [2737] (by Turk [2782] ex Kit). First and second places being taken by the dogs that James Hinks had sold to Mr Ryder, they being Old Victor [2791] and Madman [2749].

The Ninth Dog Show held at Curzon Hall in Birmingham in the first week of December 1868 showed that, in Bull Terriers, James Hinks was not in the cards. The large size class being won by Mr Bennett's Young Charlie (by Butler's Charlie ex Peter's Kiss), 2nd was Mr Ryder's Victor [2791] whilst the small size class was taken by Mr Godfree's Nelson and 2nd, Mr Aldington's Billy [2720] (by Willock's Billy out of Patch, said to be a mark eyed bitch). In Bulldogs, James Hinks won a special prize for the best Bulldog under 24lbs in the show. This was Ben [2589] (said to be by Nelson [2639] out of Wasp, although the dates of birth of Ben and Nelson make this pedigree impossible. It is more likely that the sire was Lord Nelson [2637]). In the Bulldog classes, the winner was Mr Ward's Captain, bred by Mr Lamphier and 2nd was Mr Page's Dan. In the Bulldog bitch class, James Hinks was 2nd with Rush [2712] (home bred by Crib [2605] out of Wasp). Again the dates of birth of Rush and Crib make this pedigree very suspect. The winner was Mr Lawrence's Nettle, who was a granddaughter of Hinks' Lord Nelson.

The First Exhibition of the National Dog Club was held in the Dairy Yard, Liverpool Road, Islington, in the first week in June 1869. In Bull Terriers (large size), 1st was Mr Ryder's Victor [2791], 2nd was James Hinks with another Young Madman [2742] born in 1866 (by Old Madman ex Kit) and 3rd was Mr Ryder's Puss [2823] born in 1865 (by Madman ex Puss). In the under 15lbs class, 1st was Mr Godfree's Nelson [2758], 2nd, Mr Adlington's Billy [2720], 3rd was Mr Shirley's Dick [2730] born in 1865 (by Old Dazzler ex Richards Lady). James Hinks was third in small size bulldogs with Wasp (age 18 months by Ben ex Beauty) and was also in the cards with a Toy Terrier called Fuss.

At the Tenth Dog Show, Birmingham, in late November/early December 1869, James Hinks finally turned tabled on Victor, who by then was in the ownership of Mr Smith, with Young Madman [2742] pushing Victor [2791] into second place. In small size Bull Terriers, 1st was Mr Adlington's Billy [2720] and 2nd was Mr Shirley's Nelson [2758] (again bred by Mr Willock by Stoke's, formerly Potter's, Billy ex Willock's Julia). The catalogue shows that Mr Royds exhibited his home bred bull terrier, "Tiger" and again gave good meticulous detail of the pedigree: *"Tiger" aged 2 years. By Charlie – Lill; Charlie by Madman – Lady; Madman by Mr Hinks' Madman – Old Puss; Old Puss by Rebel – Wasp; Rebel by Kit – Daisy; Wasp by Bustle – Fly. £1,000.* The Bulldog classes showed that James Hinks was still keen, gaining a highly commended with Young Dick (by King Dick ex Topsy, Topsy by Hinks' Crib).

At the Ninth Dog Show held in the Zoological Gardens, Manchester in December 1869, the Bull Terrier classes were split. In dogs, 1st was Mr Wren's Crib [2626] (breeding not given), 2nd was Mr Moore's Madman [2745] (bred by James Hinks in 1866 by Old Madman ex Puss) and 3rd was Mr Lomas with Teddy [2778] (breeding not given). In bitches, the Judge Alfred George favoured James Hinks' stock and he took the first three places. 1st was Puss [2823] (by Madman ex Puss), this bitch had also been in the ownership of Mr Ryder, who had shown her at Islington earlier in the year, 2nd was Daisy [2802] (homebred in 1868 by Madman ex Old Daisy). The KC Stud Book has her placed third but this would appear to be incorrect. 3rd was Nettle [2818] (born in 1867 by Old Madman ex Old Puss) again, the KC Stud Book has her placed second but this would appear to be incorrect. In the Bulldog classes, James Hinks gained a third place with Dick [2613] (born in 1868 by King Dick ex Topsy).

The First Grand Exhibition of sporting and other dogs, Crystal Palace, in June 1870, was organised by Mr Shirley and a group of other like minded gentlemen. However, the show was not a financial success and the gentlemen had to make up the shortfall from their own pockets. Mr Shirley would go on to be one of the founders of the Kennel Club in 1873.

At the Crystal Palace show, Mr Smith went through the cards with the dogs and bitches that he had bought from Mr Ryder. In the large size Bull Terrier class Victor [2791] was first and also won a special prize, Young Rebel [2770] was second. In bitches, 1st was Daisy [2804] (by Rebel out of Puss) and 2nd was Young Puss [2824]. In the small class, first prize and a special prize for the best bull terrier in the show was awarded to Mr Shirley's Dick [2730] (by Old Dazzler out of Richard's Lady, by Glass's Dudley out of J Tailby's Nothing). Dick had previously been in the ownership of James Hinks, Mr Swann and Mr Godfree. Mr Shirley also took first and second in bitches with Jenny [2808] (by Wild's Dick out of Kit) and Kit [2812] (by Shirley's Nelson [2758] ex Dinah, Dinah was a litter sister to Shirley's Dick). James Hinks's name did not appear in the cards in any breed at this show.

The Eleventh Dog Show, Birmingham, in late November 1870, was to prove a watershed for the organisers who, having initially been ahead of the game, did not appear to keep up with the fast pace of dog show developments. They had been slow to put on classes for bull terriers and also slow to adopt the up to date practices of large scale events. In November 1870 an open letter was published in the Birmingham Daily Gazette: *We the undersigned have not entered any dogs at Birmingham this year for the following reasons:-*

> *Because hitherto the dogs have been judged on their benches, a system which we consider fallacious in principle and unfair to exhibitors;*
>
> *Because we consider the judging should take place in public, as tending to give more confidence and cause less dissatisfaction as to the awards;*
>
> *Because we consider that in order that the dogs may be seen in their most natural forms they should, as far as possible, be led out by their own keepers and that those who do not send keepers should not practically disqualify the dogs of those who do, thus placing the whole in a position that they cannot be properly judged;*
>
> *Because we intend to support only those shows where the dogs in each class are led out together to an open space or ring and judged in the presence of the public, as is carried out at the following places: London, Darlington, Birkenhead, Manchester, Middleton, Wigan, Lancaster, Rochdale, Carlisle, Penrith, etc and similar to the practice at all Horse, Cattle and Poultry Shows.*

The letter continued in similar vein from those who had entered this year's show but said they would not do so again until the practices changed in line with those adopted by other shows. The names under the letter included Mr Royds of Rochdale and Mr Lamphier of bulldog fame. It was also stated that a large number of exhibitors agreed with the letter but did not wish their names disclosed.

At the Birmingham show, whilst James Hinks did not have an entry in the Bull Terrier Classes, he did, exhibit and win an extra prize with a cropped bulldog, imported from France, and bred by his dog dealer associate, Mr Bult, of Paris. This dog, Crib, born in 1869 was said to be by a Bordeaulais bulldog. James Hinks also exhibited a Black and Tan Terrier, a Toy Terrier and a 2 year old French Night Dog. In the Bull Terrier classes, Mr Smith again took the large class with Victor [2791] and Mr Shirley the small class with Dick [2730].

The final show of 1870 was the Tenth Dog Show, held in the Zoological Gardens, Manchester. In Bull Terriers, the dog class was won by Mayhew's Victor [2789] (by Old Victor [2791] ex Willock's Features); 2nd was Mr Lomas with Teddy (no breeding given). The small size (under 16lbs) class was won by Mr Shirley's Nelson [2758]; 2nd Mr Aldington's Billy [2720]. James Hinks's name did not appear in the cards in any breed at this show.

The Second Grand Exhibition of sporting and other dogs, Crystal Palace, in June 1871 was more or less a repeat of the 1870 show, with Mr Smith again going through the cards with the dogs and bitches that he had bought from Mr Ryder. There was a champion class, won by Rebel [2770] with Victor [2791] second. In the bitch champion class, Puss [2824] took the prize. In the open class, we see Mr Lamphier trying his hand and winning with Tiney [2779] (by Tiny ex Rose) and 2nd was Mrs Nightingale with Madman [2747] (said to be by a son of Victor out of a Deaf Sam bitch). In the small size champion classes, Mr Shirley took all the prizes with his champion dogs Nelson [2758] and Dick [2730] and his bitch Jenny [2808] (by Wild's Dick ex Kit). Mr Shirley also took the prize in the open class with Triton [2781] (by Nelson ex Jenny).

At the Twelfth Dog Show at Birmingham in December 1871, Mr Smith remained at the forefront in large bull terriers, with Rebel [2770] first and Victor [2791] second. Mr Smith was also highly commended with Madman and Puss. In small size Bull Terriers, Mr Godfree was first with Nelson [2752]. Mr Godfree would later sell this dog to Mr Shirley who changed its name to Dick II, 2nd was Mr Summer's Rebel [2771], previously owned by Mr Shirley.

James Hinks Exhibits Again

However, James Hinks could not resist a final flourish in Bull Terriers at the last major show in 1871, that being Manchester, 28th to 30th December, when he did have something to shout about. James Hinks again reigned supreme with the pups he obtained from the Mayhew's Victor/Steele's Puss litter. White Prince [2760] took first prize and Rebel [2769] was third. He also took second place with Turk [2782] (born in 1866, by Rebel ex Fly).

However, this was not a one off as James Hinks exhibited and won with White Prince and Rebel at other shows during 1872, as reported in the Birmingham Daily Post on 31st August: Bingley Dog Show – *We see from the Manchester papers that Mr J Hinks of Worcester Street, the well known breeder of dogs, has carried off several prizes at this show. In the bull- terrier class his White Prince, as a matter of course, took first prize. Prince is without exception the noblest dog of his class we have ever seen and may challenge the world. The second prize was carried off by the same gentleman's White Rebel, a descendant of his celebrated Madman, which Stonehenge regards as the perfection of a bull-terrier. In the black and tan (toy) terrier bitch class he also carried off the first prize and in the variety class was third with a very handsome Pug.*

Also on 23rd September 1872: The Middleton Dog Show – *this great dog show was held last week and proved a brilliant success; the different classes being represented by some of the best dogs in the country. Bulldogs introduced three entirely new to the neighbourhood, Mr Hinks (of Birmingham) taking first with Crib, a splendid animal.....Mr Hinks also took first and second in a very strong class of Bull-terriers, with his unrivalled White Prince and Rebel.....The Toy Terriers were very good.....Mr Hinks and Mr Morris were equal second.*

Around this time, for reasons that can, at the moment, only be guessed at, Fred who was then aged 19 took off to Manchester with White Prince and Rebel. I believe that there may be two plausible explanations for this. Perhaps James Hinks was considering selling the dogs (we will probably never know). Another possibly more plausible reason being, perhaps, that following the Ashton dog stealing case and James Hinks's dealings with the lowlife Smith, which affected his good reputation, Fred became Hinks's more reputable "man in Manchester" sending suitable dogs of all breeds from the Manchester area to his father in Birmingham for resale. So was it in Manchester that Fred honed his dog dealing skills that were to serve him so well over the coming years.

The Catalogue of The Thirteenth Birmingham Show in early December 1872 clearly showed that Fred Hinks intended to take over the mantle from his father. Fred exhibited under his own name the Mayhew's Victor/Steele's Puss litter brothers, White Prince [2760] and Rebel [2769]. His address in the catalogue was stated to be 12 South Street, Stockport Road, Ashton-Under-Lyne. Neither James Hinks nor James Jr appeared in the list of exhibitors at this Birmingham show. Could Fred taking off with his father's two best dogs have been the cause of the rift which appears to have developed between the two brothers. South Street in Ashton-Under-Lyne has been mainly redeveloped but the old railway station at the end of South Street (now called Guide Bridge Station) is still standing. The railway station in the same road where Fred lived would give him easy access to the rail network between Manchester, Birmingham and London and Manchester and Sheffield. This would have been ideal for Fred to send his dogs to shows and to send dogs from the Manchester area to his father for resale.

James Hinks continued to show his Bulldogs as confirmed by a report in the Birmingham Daily Post on the local Hanley Poultry and Dog show held in February 1873, which appears to disclose that James Hinks and both his sons were all exhibitors at the show: *In Bulldogs, Mr James Hinks of Worcester Street took first prize with his dog Crib, by the celebrated Sheffield dog Tumbler..... In the Bull Terrier class...the first and second prizes were awarded to Mr Frederick Hinks of Ashton-Under-Lyne with his White Prince and Rebel....... In class 40 (best bull terrier which has not taken a prize) Mr J Hinks was first with Young Prince...and a brother of the same dog was highly commended.*

At the Nottingham show in 1873, James Hinks of 53 Worcester Street, Birmingham took second place with a home bred Bull Terrier called Napper [2751] (by Rebel ex Kit) and at the Nottingham show in 1874, the Kennel Club Stud Book shows that Mr J Hinks of 53 Worcester Street, Birmingham gained an entry with the Bulldog Lord Nelson [4552] for a second prize. He also gained an entry with an under 18lbs Bull Terrier bitch, Countess [4593] (by Gambler ex Little Puss) also for a second prize. James Jr did not live at 53 Worcester Street at that time, so he could not have been the exhibitor. Fred was third in his class with White Prince, where he stood behind Mr Yardley's Bill [2719] and Mr Hughes' Madman [4579] (by Ryder's Madman ex Puss). Fred promptly sold White Prince to Mr Dawes of Leamington, who showed the dog at Birmingham, also taking the third prize.

During 1874, James Hinks again sold his kennel of Bull Terriers, this time to Mr R J Hartley of Altrincham. The dogs sold to Mr Hartley included Daisy [6601], Young Turk [6599] and his litter sister Countess [6600] (by Young Gambler ex Old Daisy). Countess was to become an important brood bitch, being the mother of one of the key sires of the breed, that being Dutch [13818], bred by Mr Hartley and owned by Fred Hinks.

Following the death of James Hinks, Mrs Hinks also had a clear out with no less than thirteen bull terriers changing hands. These sales brought an important name to the fore, that of Mr J R Pratt of Stoke on Trent. Mr Pratt was to set himself up nicely with dogs of Hinks's breeding. From Mrs Hinks he bought Viking [9522] whelped in 1877 (by Young Victor ex Herloin). Young Victor was sired by Mark Eyed Victor and Herloin was by Victor (Old Victor ex Puss) out of Countess (Young Gambler ex Old Daisy). He also acquired Myrtle [7631] (no breeding given), Noble [8598] bred by Hinks in 1877 (by Old Victor ex Daisy, Daisy by White Prince ex Puss) and Prince [8600] bred by Hinks (by White Prince ex Puss). From Mr Hartley, he bought Turk [8607] bred by Hinks in 1876 (by Hood's Turk ex Nell); Little Jim [7612] bred by Hinks in 1874 (by Bertie ex Fly) and Kit (by Dick out of an unregistered bitch).

Hinks – The Next Generation

Both James Hinks's sons, James Jr and Fred were actively involved in Bull Terriers. In 1871, James Jr was in lodgings with Mrs Sharp in Lower Hurst Street and he then married Annie Chester in 1872. In 1877 they were resident at the Bird in Hand tavern, Sandpits Lane, Birmingham. Their address in 1880 was 86 Spring Hill, Birmingham and by 1881, they lived at The Clown in Pershore Street, Birmingham, James Jr being described in official documents as a "Beer Retailer". In 1886, James Jr fell into a little bother with the law. He was by then the landlord of the Red Cow Inn, Horse Fair, Birmingham and was summoned for assaulting Thomas Gallagher, a labourer. Apparently, James Jr lent Mr Gallagher money to spend in his hostelrie. Mr Gallagher gladly took up the offer to quaff the "free" ale but then declined to repay James Jr the money. James Jr was fined 20 shillings and ordered to pay costs. By 1891 Annie Hinks had, in good style, produced 8 children. The family by then lived in Worcester Street, St Martins, Birmingham and James Jr was described as a "General Dealer".

Whilst James Jr did appear to show bull terriers, it was 1876 before The Kennel Club Stud Book showed the first clear mention of James Jr, as a breeder of a bull terrier called Beadle [5490], *bred by "J. Hinks Jun", whelped in 1874.* Beadle was sired by White Prince [2760] out of Puss (by Old Victor out of Puss).

The following is an extract from a narrative description by James Jr penned for the American magazine "Dogdome"in the early 1930's about the creation of the new breed by his father. At the time of wring, James Jr would be in his eighties. Whilst the narrative is very detailed we should, perhaps, remember that James Jr was born in 1851 and would only be a young child during the period that he is recalling:

The all white Bull-terrier was founded by my father, James Hinks, of Birmingham... My father died in 1878 and after his death I carried on until some few years ago I handed over the reins to my son, Carleton.... The forbears of my father's dogs presented a comical appearance, with their short thick heads, blunt muzzles, showing a certain amount of Bulldog layback, bow legs, thick set bodies and overhanging lips, whilst in colour they varied between black and tan, brindle, red, fallow, etc. They were known as Bull and Terriers, owing to their being a cross between the Bulldog and a Terrier, the latter being chiefly the large Black and Tan Terrier and any Terrier which showed gameness and a nose for rats was used in the crossing. They were queer looking dogs, being neither Bulldog nor Terrier; however, they served the purpose they were bred for, ie fighting, ratting, badger and bull baiting..... The cross was ideal, as the strength of the Bulldog was united with the quickness and intelligence of the Terrier....

Around the end of the 1850's a great change came about: My father, who had previously owned some of the gamest of the old stock with which he had been experimenting and crossing with the White English Terrier and Dalmatian, bred a strain of all-white dogs, which he called Bull-terriers, by which name they became duly recognised.

These dogs were refined and their Bulldog appearance being still further bred out, they were longer and cleaner in head, stronger in foreface, free from lippiness and throatiness and necks were longer; they became more active; in short they became the old fighting dog civilized, with all his rough edges smoothed down without being softened; alert, active, plucky, muscular and a real gentleman. Naturally, this change brought the Bull-terrier many admirers and the milk white dog became the fashion.

In James Jr's article he makes no mention of his brother Fred in relation to carrying on the work of their father, nor to the development of the breed and neither does his son Carleton in Carleton's writings on the breed. This would, perhaps, indicate a family rift? As we have seen above and further below, it was Fred who clearly took over the mantle of his Father. This is evidenced by the Kennel Club Stud Book, records and champions. From these it would certainly show without any doubt whatsoever that Fred Hinks was the one who very immediately carried on the work of his father in relation to Bull

Terriers. Rawdon B Lee attested that *between Mr A George of London and Fred Hinks of Birmingham must be divided the honour attending the reputation of being the largest dealers in Bull Terriers in the Country.* In his book "The Bull Terrier" published in 1912, William Haynes writes that *James Hinks, the father, and Fred Hinks, his son, made Birmingham the centre of the breed.* Interestingly, there is no mention of James Jr. In "The Dog Book" published in 1906, the American writer James Watson attests that *Birmingham was the city where the show bull terrier was brought to perfection. Most of the good imported dogs have been from that district and the largest exporter to this Country is Fred Hinks of that city.* Drury in British Dogs, published in 1903, comments that *of those breeders at present before the public who have done great service in endeavouring to popularise this game British dog, Mr F Hinks........may be especially named,* again, no mention of James Jr.

Fred Hinks, at the age of 25, married Anne Prosser Reading in 1878, the same year of his father's death. They lived in Bath Row, St Thomas, Birmingham and, at the time, Fred was a "General Clerk". Fred was stated in the KC Stud Book in 1883 to be an Associate of the Kennel Club. By 1891, Fred was described as a "Beerhouse Keeper" and, in 1893 lived at 117 Bristol Street, Birmingham. By 1901, the family lived in Ryland Road, Edgbaston, Birmingham and Fred was described in official documents as a "Canine Dealer". Fred died on 14th January 1914, leaving his estate, valued at £37.14s. 8d to his youngest daughter Elsie Amelia Hinks, who was aged about 23.

To see how important Fred Hinks's contribution was, let's start by looking at the premise that all Bull Terriers are related and all from the same original Hinks stock. For this we can thank Count Hollender's love of blood lines, pedigrees and his use of the "Figure System" to determine the origin of the original or common stock. The "Figure System" ignores the body of the pedigree and traces back only the top and bottom lines of the pedigree, often called the "Tail Male" (or Strain) and "Tail Female" (or family) lines.

Count Hollender recounted in his excellent book "The Bull Terrier And All About It" (1932), that in all the pedigrees he was able to expand in such manner, the "Tail male" line ended up with one of two dogs. The first was called "Short Tail" the parents of whom Count Hollender says were unregistered. The second was called "Old Victor" whose parentage was also unknown but who was said to be known to be the sire of Fred Hinks's dog "Dutch". Hinks's

Dutch sired Gladstone who, in turn, was the sire of Ch Gully the Great, a key dog in the development of the breed on both sides of the Atlantic.

Short Tail, so called due to an accident when a puppy and, consequently not shown for the same reason, was all white and born in 1888. He was owned by Fred Hinks, who offered him at stud for a fee of 1 Guinea. From research using material apparently not available to Count Hollender at the time, the sire of Short Tail was called "Vic", who was a grandson of "Dutch". Short Tail's dam was called "Violet" who was a granddaughter of "Little Victor". Therefore, it transpires that Old Victor was, in fact, the double g.g.grand sire of Short Tail. Expanding Count Hollender's Figure System, this puts "Old Victor" as the original common ancestor of the modern Bull Terrier. Old Victor's pedigree remains unknown. These dogs would have obviously gone back to the rootstock of the founder, Fred's father, James Hinks's dogs.

Conformists issue a note of caution when considering old pedigrees because, as we have seen, breeders and owners at the time were apt to use and reuse the names of successful dogs and names like "Dutch", "Victor", "Rose", "Madman", "Puss" and "Nell" were commonplace, together with the names being prefaced by "Young" and "Old". So there were many "Victor's", "Young Victor's" and "Old Victor's" etc. and dogs quite often went through several different hands. Also, an owner could change the name of a dog and there are several instances of dogs and bitches up to the mid 1950's siring or whelping litters under different names. Furthermore, it was not compulsory to register dogs and, whilst some dogs were registered, many bitches in particular remained unregistered and their pedigrees not recorded.

This confusion of dogs with the same name was seized upon by the early dog book writers and breed historians and, again, the conformists repeated that, for example, with the first KC Stud Book for 1874 showing five Puss's, six Victor's and twelve Madman *to separate one from the other.....would be impossible now.* Again, this is not so, the entries for Bull Terriers in the first KC Stud Book can quite easily be cross referenced to the detailed show reports in the same document and further cross referenced to show catalogues, dog books and to press reports of the dog shows. For example, of the six Victor's, we find that four entries relate to Old Victor [2791], one entry relates to Old Victor's son, Mayhew's Victor [2789] and one entry relates to Mayhew's Victor's son, the patched/mark eyed dog, Young Victor [2792]. The twelve Madman entries can be quite easily narrowed down by the same method to eleven different dogs (one of those actually being Young Victor, whom we have previously noted was campaigned by Mr T Moore under the name of Madman II) and the five Puss's are all different bitches. The first KC Stud Book, compiled in 1874, was a great reference book which, particularly if used in conjunction with other corroborative sources of information, helped, to a large extent, to cut through some of the confusion.

Fred Hinks had a stud card produced for Short Tail, which is reproduced below, courtesy of The Bull Terrier Club, giving provenance to its breeding. This stud card was published in the Bull Terrier Club Annual in 1951.

In Richard Glyn's book, 'Bull Terriers and How To Breed Them', he traces the main bloodlines back through Hampstead Heathen and Lord Gladiator to Ch Charlwood Victor Wild and, thereupon, further back to Short Tail. There is no doubt that Dutch, often referred to as "Hinks's Dutch" was important in the development of the breed. This dog, said to be bred by Mr R J Hartley of Altrincham and at one time in the ownership of Fred Hinks, was

Dutch, one of the recognised pillars of the breed

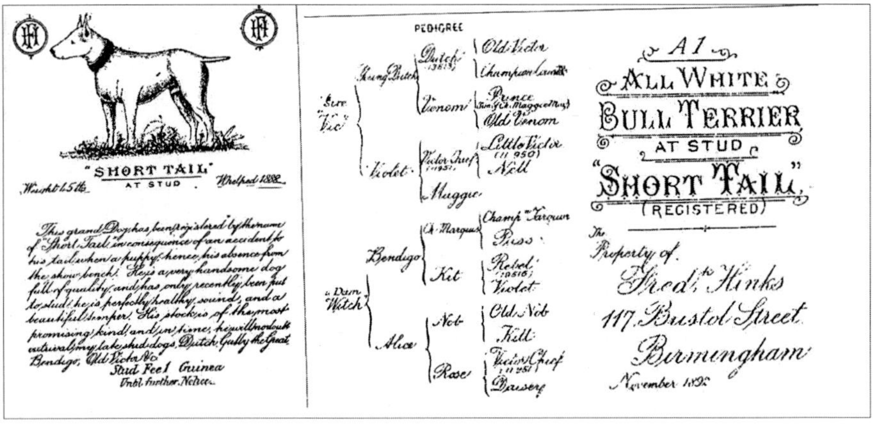

not a show dog due to his terrible front. However, he did make the KC Stud Book due to his prepotence as a sire, winning the stud dog prize at The British Kennel Association show at Aston Park, Birmingham in May 1883.

Fred Hinks bought Dutch and it is said placed the young puppy with a friend who unfortunately kept him chained up. Consequently, when Fred Hinks collected Dutch, he was drastically out at elbow. Fred nevertheless held onto the dog because he had an admirable head and used him at stud. The sire of Dutch was stated to be "Old Victor".

There are two things which I have found dismaying when reading breed history books, the first is that they often follow suit and just regurgitate the same information, quite often even using the same wording and the second is that, when faced with an apparent dead end, they make no attempt to investigate further and provide the reader with some insight into what may have happened. So Dutch, one of the recognised pillars of the breed was said to be sired by Old Victor [2791]. All the breed history books that I have read follow suit and conform that this cannot be so, repeating the mystery of Bull Terrier pedigrees and the number of dogs/bitches having the same name. They then shrug their shoulders and move on, leaving the hapless reader no better off. Dutch's dam, Countess, was not born until 1874, whereas Old Victor was found dead in his box by Rawden Lee at the Crystal Palace show in 1872. To try and get to the bottom of the matter, instead of looking at Dutch and Old Victor and scratching our heads, we should look at Dutch's mother, Countess [6600].

It is not disputed that the mother of Dutch was Countess [6600]. Countess was born in 1874 and whelped a litter in 1875. This litter contained a dog, Marquis [6592] and a bitch, Magnet [6608] and they were sired by none other than "Victor". In addition, we have seen above that Countess also whelped a litter which contained a bitch called Herloin (sired by Old Victor). Could it be then but there can be no certainty or verification of this, that Dutch was out of one of these two litters. The KC Stud Book for 1883 only gives a guestimate of Dutch's date of birth as *about six years old.* Which "Victor" was the sire? Certainly not Old Victor [2791] who died in 1872. So which other Victors' does that leave us with. We have only two real possibilities, they being Young Victor, the mark eyed dog [2792] and his sire, referred to above, Mayhew's Victor [2789]. Which of these Victor's was the sire of Dutch, we may probably never know. Suffice it to say that Old Victor was the sire of Mayhew's Victor and thereby the grandsire of Young Victor, the "Tail Male" bloodline of Dutch remains the same.

Ch Gully the Great

To emphasise the difficulty that the early writers experienced, the pedigree for Ch Gully the Great stated in Hogarth's book "The Bull Terrier" is incorrect, as confirmed by my own research with the Kennel Club and great thanks to Bill Lambert and Ciara Farrell at the KC Library for their help in this respect. The correct pedigree for Ch Gully the Great is given below, from which it will be noted that he was the result of a half brother half sister mating to the prepotent Ch Maggie May. Ch Gully the Great carried a tan mark to one side of his face.

Ch Gully the Great, influential on both sides of the Atlantic

<table>
<tr><td rowspan="8">Ch Gully The Great</td><td rowspan="4">Hinks's Gladstone</td><td rowspan="2">Hinks's Dutch</td><td>Old Victor</td></tr>
<tr><td>Countess</td></tr>
<tr><td rowspan="2">Ch Maggie May</td><td>Old Prince</td></tr>
<tr><td>Kit</td></tr>
<tr><td rowspan="4">Florrie</td><td rowspan="2">Baron</td><td>Hinks's Dutch</td></tr>
<tr><td>Lucy</td></tr>
<tr><td rowspan="2">Ch Maggie May</td><td>Old Prince</td></tr>
<tr><td>Kit</td></tr>
</table>

Ch Gully the Great was owned by Fred Hinks who exported him to Mr F Dole in America in 1891. If Fred Hinks was the biggest dealer and exporter of bull terriers, then Mr Dole matched him as the biggest importer and dealer. Mr Dole imported many Bull Terriers and from two such imports, Ch Grand Duke (by Dutch ex Young Magnet) and Ch Maggie May, he bred the unbeaten American Ch Starlight.

Fred Hinks owned, amongst others the stud dogs, Dutch, Bendigo, Cairo and Gully the Great. Yes, for the most part, these are now just names but let us not forget that Ch Gully the Great became a key dog both sides of the Atlantic. In fact we can now say that Ch Gully the Great was the starting point of a slow change of breeding influence.

Ch Maggie May

The dogs in Ch Gully the Great's pedigree also show the pre eminence of the Hinks bloodline over the first 30 years of the breed's existence. Ch Maggie May was bred by Mr J Pratt in 1879. She was sired by Hinks' Old Prince out of Kit (by Dick out of an unregistered bitch) and became a champion in 1884. In 1881 Ch Magnet had been made up. She was bred by Mr R J Hartley, sired by Hinks' Old Prince out of Kit (by Dick out of an unregistered bitch). So after Ch Magnet was born it looks like Mr Hartley sold Kit to Mr Pratt who promptly repeated the Old Prince/Kit mating with great success.

Ch Maggie May was the goose that laid the golden eggs and certainly she was phenomenal in the whelping box producing over the next few years no less than 5 UK champion offspring to different sires. This was a record which would stand for some 80 years until surpassed by Ch Souperlative Summer Queen producing seven UK champion offspring. Summer Queen was fortunate because she may not have achieved this record had Maggie May remained in the Country. There is no doubt that Ch Maggie May would have produced further UK champions as when, at the age of eight, she was exported to America, she went on to produce two American champion litter sisters, Ch Attraction and the unbeaten Ch Starlight.

Ch Maggie May's first champion son was Max Marx, bred by Mr Pratt, who had used Fred Hinks' "Dutch" on her. In 1886, Mr Alfred George's Cairo became a champion. Ch Cairo was sired by Ch Max Marx out of Ch Mistress of the Robes, so this was a full brother to sister mating. Cairo was at one time owned by Fred Hinks who sold him on to Mr Chatwin of Birmingham prior to Alfred George coming into his possession. Alfred George exported Ch Cairo to Mr Hobbie in the States. Ch Mistress of the Robes, bred by Mr Pratt, was by Fred Hinks' Dutch out of Ch Maggie May and this was therefore the result of a half brother half sister mating. Ch Mistress of the Robes litter sister, Ch Queen of the May, was also made up in 1886. There was no doubt that Mr Pratt was having a fine old time, making up three champions in the same year, two of which were litter mates.

Mr Pratt appears to have then sold Ch Maggie May to Mr H Whitehead, who promptly put a son of Fred Hinks' Dutch, called Baron, on her and was rewarded with Ch Como gaining his title in 1890 and giving Ch Maggie May her fourth champion offspring. Ch Como's litter sister was Florrie who became the mother of Ch Gully the Great. Ch Maggie May appears to then have been sold to Mr J F Fielding who mated her to another "Dutch" (parents unregistered) and she produced her fifth UK champion Trentham Dutch. Ch Trentham Dutch had a fawn ear but was still able to win at the highest level. Fred Hinks used Ch Trentham Dutch on his bitch Countess, producing another good dog in the KC Stud book, though not a champion, called Holland.

The important sire, Streatham Monarch, by Streatham Flyer (a son of Ch Gully the Great) out of Trentham Baroness (by Trentham Dutch) was born in 1889. He gained his title in 1891and went to the States in the same year, to John Moorehead of Pittsburgh. Mr Moorehead also imported Queen Bendigo (by Bendigo ex Mag) and Mister Dick (by Young Dutch ex Nettle).

Fred Hinks bred Ch Greenhill Wonder by Gladstone ex Nell. Nell was sired by Rebel out of Nelly. This bitch, a half sister to Ch Gully the Great, was owned by the Lea brothers who made her a champion in 1890 and, along with the Trentham dogs, were one of the first to use a prefix. In 1894 the Lea's made up Ch Faultless by Duke of Marlborough out of Nance. Duke of Marlborough was sired by Fred Hinks's Bendigo (Ch Marquis ex Kit) and was to prove to be an excellent sire. In the same year the Lea's also made up Ch Greenhill

Beatrice who was sired by Ladywood Prince (a son of Ch Gully the Great) out of Greenhill Bess. Greenhill Bess was a daughter of Modesty. Modesty, who became a champion in 1894 was the litter sister to Ch Faultless and was owned by Fred Hinks. Ch White Wonder, who also gained her title in 1894, was sired by Ch Gully the Great. In that year another Duke of Marlborough son, Ch Grand Prior, also gained his title.

The Bull Terrier went from strength to strength, overcoming its riff raff image to become the gentleman's friend and with exports serving to put the breed on the map in other countries, particularly America, where the Americans really took to the breed as if it were their own.

Ear Cropping in England and America

The Bull Terrier Club in England was formed in 1887 and BTCA was formed in 1895. Both became mired in the ear cropping debate in their respective countries, with widely different results. Breeders of Irish Terriers also took a hand in the debate in both countries, again with widely different results. The movement against ear cropping had come to prominence at the Islington show in June 1862 when Sir Edwin Landseer advocated that *in future no dogs with cropped ears, or otherwise mutilated, shall be admitted into shows.* Some 27 years later, the Irish Terrier Club in England petitioned the Kennel Club to have an ear cropping ban introduced solely for their own breed. This was granted by the Kennel Club and it was ruled that *No Irish Terrier born after 31st December 1889, can, if cropped, win a prize at any show held under Kennel Club Rules.* With this partial success under their belts, the anti croppers were able to apply more pressure towards the fulfilment of their aims and it was to be an Irish Terrier that brought matters to a head in 1895.

Mr and Mrs Carling were summoned to appear in Court for cruelty to a dog, in that they had cut off the dogs ears. This was not a Bull Terrier but an Irish Terrier. Nevertheless, the Bull Terrier Club saw fit not only to contribute 8 guineas towards the Carling's defence but also to give evidence on their behalf. The Carlings were convicted. King Edward VII, who was patron of the Kennel Club, apparently penned a letter to the effect that in his opinion the practise of the cropping of dogs ears must stop. As a result, the Kennel Club introduced the prohibition of ear cropping which determined that a dog with cropped ears could not be a prize winner – *no dog born after 31st March 1895 should, if cropped, win a prize at any show held under Kennel Club rules.*

At the time this brought to an end the fortunes of the breed in England which commenced on a downward spiral as neither breeders nor the public took to an uncropped Bull Terrier. Americans were not so hindered as cropping remained and the breed continued to grow in popularity Stateside. There were, of course, attempts to introduce a ban on cropping in America. Whilst in England, the King's requirement was immediately implemented, things were very different in the States.

The Bull Terrier Club of America was admitted to membership of the American Kennel Club at its meeting on 12th September 1895. This was proven to be somewhat fortuitous because just three months later, at a special meeting of the AKC, held on 19th December 1895, a proposed Constitutional rule was put forward prohibiting a dog that has been cropped to be shown. There were 19 members present, 11 voting for the proposed ban and 8 voting against. However, a two thirds majority was required, so the proposal was defeated. This narrow defeat obviously left a bitter taste on both sides. We are indebted to the American Kennel Club Library & Archives for allowing extracts of the AKC minutes to be reproduced.

Dr H T Foote, an associate member of the AKC, wrote of the matter in the December 1895 issue of the Kennel Gazette and proposed a further resolution *Whereas the mutilation of dogs is a recognised cruelty and not necessary or justifiable, except in cases of diseas, and whereas, the cruelty animal laws through out of States make such mutilation a misdemeanour punishable by imprisonment and fine, Resolve: that all dogs born after December 31st 1895 must be shown in their natural conditions, and if in any way mutilated will be considered improperly tampered with, and subject to the rules governing Bench Shows.* Such rules called for the judge to disqualify dogs that had perceived to have been tampered with. The matter was apparently discussed at the BTCA meeting held on 13th January 1896 and certain action resolved to be taken against Dr Foote, his co presenter Mr Schellhass and others who may choose to support another resolution to ban cropping. The proposed action included taking out newspaper adverts across the Country naming and shaming those delegates who were in favour of a ban on cropping. Mr Dole, president of BTCA denied any wrongdoing, saying that the BTCA meeting was merely held to consider the offering of special prizes at its shows.

Details of the altercation were contained in the AKC's secretary's quarterly report. This included a statement from Mr Schellhass (National Beagle Club): *This communication I consider was meant to act an intimidation to the delegates either in discussing this cropping question or as to their votes and for that reason I felt it my duty to request the American Kennel Club to assert its protection to the delegates.* This was supported by Mr Burritt (Boston Terrier Club) *Personally I must admit that I consider such a resolution and spread broadcast by the Bull Terrier Club not only as unjust, unreasonable but almost a direct slap at the American Kennel Club.*

An amendment to Mr Foote's proposal was made and accepted *That all dogs born after June 30th 1896 must be shown with their ears in their natural condition and if in any way mutilated they will be considered improperly tampered with and subject to the rules governing bench shows.* Mr Brooks (New England Kennel Club) correctly pointed out that the resolution proposed would be of no effect because what was being proposed was not a change to the bench show rules, requiring only a majority in favour but was a Constitutional amendment requiring a two thirds majority and such a proposed amendment to the Constitution had been recently voted on and failed and was likely to fail again. Mr Brooks's opinion held sway because, after considerable further discussion, it appeared to be the consensus that such a resolution to change the bench show rules would be inoperative and Dr Foote withdrew it. However, Mr Schellhass persisted, proposing that the matter be brought up at the next meeting of the AKC. Mr Schellhass's proposal was defeated by twelve votes to six.

Irish Terrier breeders in the States entered the fray, sending a petition to AKC to make a ruling to debar all cropped Irish Terriers, whelped after January 1st 1897, from competing at shows held under AKC rules However, they were at a disadvantage to their English counterparts in that no club had been formed for Irish Terriers in the States. The matter was discussed at the AKC meeting on 17th September 1896, with Dr Foote inevitably in support. Again, there were mixed views with Mr Burritt (Boston Terrier Club) advising that the request was outside the province of the AKC and Mr Blossom (Gordon Setter Club) saying that the request by the Irish Terrier breeders should be granted. Mr Watson (Collie Club of America) perhaps saved the day by proposing that if the Irish Terrier breeders wished to debar cropped Irish Terriers from being shown, then they should rightly form a club and adopt that as part of its standard. Mr Watson's proposal was accepted and the Irish Terrier breeders informed accordingly.

So ended the attempt to introduce an ear cropping ban in the States at that time. However, the defeated delegates would seek retribution for the actions of BTCA and its officers. At a committee meeting of the AKC, held on 11th April 1896, it was resolved that the committee of BTCA take certain actions as a consequence of the intimidatory proposals towards delegates who supported a ban on ear cropping. BTCA did not reply. At the Quarterly meeting of the AKC held on 21st May 1896 where, in the absence of both the president and vice president, Mr Foote was elected as the presiding officer, it was *ORDERED That the Bull Terrier Club of America be and is hereby granted fifteen (15) days, within which to comply with the resolution of this committee, adopted at its meeting held April 11, 1896, in default of which said club, and its officers, holding office on January 13, 1896 shall be thereby suspended.* BTCA did not reply, nor comply, with the resolution of the committee of the AKC and was suspended. Mr Dole and Mr Moorehead, being two of the officers were also suspended. Both gentlemen appealed. Mr Moorehead (the owner of Ch Streatham Monarch) was reinstated after severing ties with BTCA and Mr Dole's appeal was referred to the Advisory committee. The suspension had consequences for BTCA, in that Clubs affiliated to the AKC were prevented from accepting prizes offered to them by BTCA at their benched shows.

The club remained suspended for over a year and, in April 1897, the Secretary of AKC was instructed to write to BTCA to show cause why it should not be expelled for conduct *prejudicial to the interests of the American Kennel Club.* Again, BTCA did not reply to this correspondence and on 20th May 1897 the club was dropped from the role of AKC membership. Following this there must, perhaps, have been some serious back room politicking going on because BTCA was accepted as a new member of AKC on 24th November 1897. The proposed action to ban cropping did not materialise. The 1936 revised Standard for the Bull Terrier still referred to a cropped or uncropped ear and this remained the case until 1957, when reference to cropping was removed.

Bibliography and Notes

Numbers in parenthesis [ ] refer to KC Stud Book numbers

Books:

A History and Description of the Modern Dogs of Great Britain (Lee)

A Journey into England (Hentzner)

American Kennel Register

Batty's Descriptive Catalogue of the Copper Coinage of Great Britain

Bentley's Miscellany

Birmingham Dog Show Society Catalogue 1860, courtesy of the Kennel Club Library

British Dogs (Dalziel)

British Dogs (Drury)

British Terriers (Maxtee)

Bull Terriers (Hollender)

Bull Terrier of Today (BTCA)

Bull Terriers and how to breed them (Glyn)

Crufts Catalogues, courtesy of the Kennel Club Library

Decanibus Britannicis (Caius, translator Fleming)

Dogs and All About Them (Leighton)

Dog Shows and Doggy People (Lane)

Exposition Universelle Des Races Canines Catalogue 1863

Forty Years of Bull Terriers (Adlam)

From Little Acorns – History of Birmingham Championship Show
History of My Own Times (Burnet)
Illustrations of Typical Dogs (Drury)
Made in Birmingham (Harris)
Manchester Dog Show Catalogues, Courtesy of Manchester City Library
Pardon's Book
Pity Me (Kane)
Real Life in London
Researches into the History of the British Dog (Jesse)
Rural Sports (Daniel)
Survey of London (Stow)
The American Book of the Dog (Sheilds)
The American Kennel Club Stud Books
The Bulldog (Meyer)
The Bulldog A Monograph (Farman)
The Bull Terrier (Haynes)
The Bull Terrier (Montgomery)
The Bull Terrier and all about it (Hollender)
The Complete Dog Book (Bruette)
The Dog (Idestone)
The Dog Book (Watson)
The Dogs of the British Islands (Stonehenge)
The Dogs of Great Britain, America and Other Countries (Stonehenge)
The Everyday Book of Popular Amusements (Hone)
The Idestone Papers
The Illustrated Book of the Dog (Shaw)
The Kennel Club Calendar and Stud Books
The Kennel Encyclopaedia (Barton)
The New Book of the Dog (Leighton)
The Practical Dog Book (Ash)
The Sporting Bull Terrier (Glass)

The Sporting Dictionary (Taplin)

The Sporting Repository (John)

Toy Dogs and their Ancestors (Lytton)

Websites:

www.akc.org

www.ancestry.co.uk

www.archive.org

www.britishnewspaperarchive.co.uk

www.bodleian.ox.ac.uk

www.chestofbooks.com

www.europeana.eu

www.gutenberg.org

www.hathitrust.org

www.instituteofcaninebiology.org

www.newspaperarchive.com

www.thekennelclub.org.uk

www.trove.nla.gov.au

www.us.archive.org

www.worldlibrary.org

www.worldofcoins.eu

Newspapers and Magazines

Transcripts from the undermentioned newspapers quoted in the book:

Aris's Birmingham Gazette

Birmingham Daily Post

Birmingham Daily Gazette

Birmingham Journal

Bell's Life in London and Sporting Chronicle

Bell's Weekly Messenger
London Gazette
London Standard
London Morning Post
London Reynolds
Penny Illustrated Paper
Penny Newsman
Sporting Life
The Ashton Weekly Reporter and Stalybridge and Dukinfield Chronicle
The Era
The Field
The Illustrated London News
Manchester Examiner

Other Newspapers Reviewed

Berkshire Chronicle
Birmingham Mail
Blackburn Standard
Bradford Observer
Cork Examiner
Coventry Times
Coventry Standard
Coventry Herald
County Courts Chronicle
Glasgow Herald
Hereford Times
Holborn Journal
Illustrated Times
Lancashire Evening Post
Leamington Spa Courier
Leeds Intelligencer
Leeds Mercury

Leicester Journal

Liverpool Mercury

Manchester Times

Manchester Courier and Lancashire General Advertiser

Manchester Evening News

Morning Advertiser

Reynold's Newspaper

Sheffield Independent

Sheffield Daily Telegraph

Staffordshire Sentinel and Commercial & General Advertiser

The Australasian

The Country

The Illustrated Sporting and Dramatic News

The Sporting Magazine

The Sportsman

Walsall Free Press and General Advertiser

Western Daily Press

Yorkshire Gazette

Kennel Club Gazette, courtesy of the Kennel Club Library

Extracts from KC Stud Books, courtesy of the Kennel Club Library and Halson Gallery

Minutes of AKC meetings, courtesy of the American Kennel Club Library & Archives

Other: The Kennel Club Library

Library of Birmingham

British Newspaper Archive

Manchester City Library

American Kennel Club Library & Archives

Illustrations:

National Exhibition of Dogs at Birmingham 1860 – The Illustrated London News – Newspaper image © The British Library Board. All Rights Reserved, with thanks to the British Newspaper Archive www.britishnewspaperarchive.co.uk

Birmingham Dog Show Catalogue 1860 – courtesy of the Kennel Club Library

Bull Baiting Print – James Henderson Collection

Badger Baiting print – James Henderson Collection

Bear Baiting print – Author's Collection

Punch Cartoon – The Bulldog A Monograph (Farman)

Dutch – The Bull Terrier (Haynes)

Old Bulldogs – The Dogs of Great Britain and America (Stonehenge)

Grand Mechanical Pit, Boars Head, Long Acre – Illustrated Sporting News

Madman the Bull Terrier – The Practical Dog Book (Ash)

McDonald's Caledonian Club, Long Acre, Coins – Author's Collection

Young Victor (woodcut by Ludlow)

Short Tail Pedigree – courtesy of The Bull Terrier Club

Old Dutch – The Dog Book (Watson)

Ch Gully the Great – Forty Years of Bull Terriers (Adlam)

Ch Maggie May – The Dog Book (Watson)

Acknowledgements

Special thanks to: Ciara Farrell, Library and Collections Manager, The Kennel Club

William Lambert, Health & Breeder Services Manager, The Kennel Club

Les and Julie Wilson of Halson Gallery – halsongal@googlemail.com

My wife, Julie and son Elliott for putting up with me